So Now You're a ZOMBIE

[DON'T EAT THIS BOOK]

THIS HANDBOOK BELONGS TO:

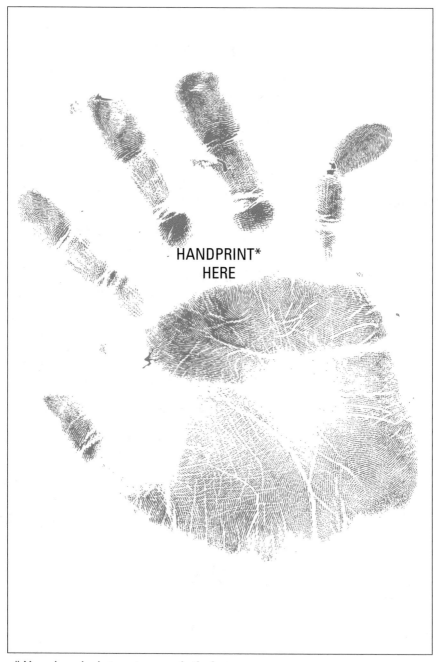

HANDPRINT*
HERE

* Your handprint, not your victim's

So Now You're a

ZOMBIE

A HANDBOOK FOR THE
NEWLY UNDEAD

JOHN AUSTIN

CHICAGO
REVIEW
PRESS

Library of Congress Cataloging-in-Publication Data

Austin, John, 1978–

So now you're a zombie : a handbook for the newly undead / John Austin.

p. cm.

ISBN 978-1-56976-342-1

1. Zombies—Humor. I. Title.

PN6231.Z65A87 2010

818'.607—dc22

2010028750

Cover and interior design: Jonathan Hahn

Illustrations: John Austin

Published by Chicago Review Press, Incorporated

814 North Franklin Street

Chicago, Illinois 60610

ISBN 978-1-56976-342-1

Printed in the United States of America

5 4 3

CONTENTS

INTRODUCTION

THE ROAD TO BRAINVILLE

For centuries, humans have stereotyped zombies as simpleminded, flesh-eating monstrosities that aimlessly stumble around the world of the living, hunting for a taste of their most precious dish: the human brain. Dripping with infected blood, zeds will slaughter, gorge, and multiply until they drive their principal food source, humankind, to extinction.

These assumptions are basically correct. We zombies are more reckless and less quick-witted than our living counterparts—our bloodstained history reflects that. But we possess other attributes and abilities that provide us with distinct advantages over the living. While our bodies are impervious to pain, humans are tormented by the slightest injury. While we lack all emotion, they are driven by pride and greed, fighting amongst themselves over resources, politics, and potential mates.

Unfortunately, humans will also fight for their own survival, hindering the ability of any zombie horde to peacefully feed on them. Most humans will run and some will hide, but few will lie down for the easy picking. Some may even battle us to the death, and it is these dead-enders who make the existence of a zombie so dangerous. A simple feeding frenzy can turn hazardous without warning, and often the zombie itself will lose an appendage—or even its head. Either outcome will hamper a zed's vile body in future feedings, and could result in its second demise.

In recent years, human resistance has been fortified by a grotesque surge in publications that outline survival strategies for the living in case of a zombie outbreak. Very few books (if any) have been written to teach brain-eaters such as you how to hunt, fight, and feed. That is precisely the reason the earth is still crawling with breathers, and why only three out of five zombies survive the first 48 hours of postmortem "life."

So Now You're a Zombie aims to correct this imbalance. Originally written in blood hundreds of years ago, it has now been updated with fresh content for today's zed. It is a digest of specific information that you, the newly undead, can absorb in order to prepare for man's brutality and improve your survival rate. If you apply its lessons instead of just eating the pages they're printed on, you'll soon become one terrorizing S.O.B.

As all zombies know, learning can be hell! But to survive, you must refocus your limited brainpower and hone what little dexterity you have left. In order to reduce the pressure on your decaying cranium, this book provides you with only the bare bones—the essential information you need to know *before* engaging with the living. *So Now You're a Zombie* will:

- Introduce you to your new smelly body
- Offer insights on the living resistance
- Provide information on how to properly attack a human
- Ensure that you feel adequately prepared to defend against last-ditch resisters
- Expose you to the nutritional demands of an all-human diet
- Provide insight from experienced zombies that have successfully infected the living
- Uncover a wide range of other issues you will face in the living world
- Outline a contingency plan for when the end is near

This information, when used correctly (and not eaten), should give you the upper hand (if still attached) over your human prey. And by reducing horde casualties, you and other well-oriented zeds can assist in the collapse of civilization. Remember, you're part of a team. When individual zombies succeed, the undead horde succeeds, and vice versa.

In short, *So Now You're a Zombie* will help you build a foundation for many aggressive, brain-gobbling years to come.

Zombie Assessment

Yes, becoming a zed can be a confusing experience. But, then, living as a human amid a zombie outbreak must be pretty bewildering as well. Who knows—maybe you're not a zombie after all! If you have any whiff of doubt about your current status, living or undead, we recommend that you use the following checklist as a self-diagnosis. Check all the boxes that apply.

- ☐ **You have a dismal appearance.** Fashion is no longer a priority, or maybe it never was. Your clothes have been reduced to rags and hang off your body. Just remember: if you are a zombie, whatever you died in is what you'll be wearing for the rest of your post-life, so hopefully you dressed comfortably.

- ☐ **You're suffering from insomnia.** Haven't slept for days, but you're still functioning? A good night's sleep has been proven to help body restoration—something every zombie will no doubt miss.

- ☐ **You notice changes in mobility.** You lack coordination and now move with a slow and shambling gait. You may experience jerks and seizures as well.

- ☐ **Communication is difficult.** Most zombies can't talk, so don't feel bad. You'll be limited to grunting and moaning—if your lungs are still intact, that is.

- ☐ **You're experiencing skin decomposition.** A zombie's skin will eventually become toxic and infectious, but in the early stages of post-life you may experience small outbreaks of flesh-eating bacteria and parasites. No reason to be alarmed; fully infected cells will quickly evict those hungry critters.

- ☐ **You've thrown off all your emotional baggage.** You have no concept of right or wrong. Awesome! Behavioral side effects may occur; they're just the tip of the iceberg.

- ☐ **Your memory is slipping.** In fact, your memory is gone! You may still find yourself being drawn toward a particular location or performing a specific action as if it's somehow familiar, but don't confuse that with memory. The body of a newly risen zed sometimes responds instinctively to certain pheromones or repeats deeply ingrained learned behavior.

- ☐ **You're bulletproof from the neck down.** Ammo may slow you down, but you are only slightly fazed by gunshots to the body. Just avoid any head shots.

☐ **You crave human brains.** Strangely, pizza and pasta no longer do it for you. The taste of ordinary human food is similar to cardboard. Vegetarian or not, you are now 100 percent carnivore.

☐ **You recently died.** This is a big one! Now you're "magically" reading this book. Spooky, huh?

If you checked only a few of the boxes (except the last one), you might still be living and uninfected; stop reading and seek professional help immediately. But if all or most of them fit the bill, you're a frickin' zombie!

So now what? Even the undead have options, however limited.

1. **Zombicide.** Find a convenient way to destroy your remaining brain function and end it all (see "Zombicide," page 140). However, you will never have the opportunity to have your boss as an appetizer.

2. **Shamble alone.** Assume that this guide carries the stench of burden. Abandon its advice and search aimlessly for a brainy brunch until someone cuts off your head.

3. **Accept your fate.** Try to extract some of the knowledge from this manual and join the struggle, uprising, plague, apocalypse . . . call it what you will!

If you moaned "*threeeeeee*," we are drooling with excitement that you crave an evil education, and will help you take those first shambling steps as a new zed.

Safety Precautions

While you drool over these pages, you must remember one thing: ***keep this book from those living bastards!*** Humans may already have access to countless volumes of zombie lore and survival strategies written by their own so-called experts, but these books are often filled with inaccurate or outdated information. Because this is an official guide by zombies, for zombies, the insights it contains would prove far more dangerous in mortal hands. Let the humans continue to believe the centuries-old myths they have prepared for.

To protect the manual, place it in one of your open body cavities for safekeeping. If in fact a human terminates you, the book and all its knowledge will be disposed of along with your corpse. An inexperienced human would never risk the chance of viral infection by touching or dissecting a zombie.

Zeds' Disclaimer

The knowledge in this book has come at a price. Thousands of relentless zombies have given up their post-lives to amass it. It is important to remember, however, that the zombies who wrote this book possessed questionable intelligence. Even with their limited IQs pooled together, some information in this book might prove incomplete or misleading. If you choose to apply the principles outlined in this book, your safety and the safety of the horde are not guaranteed.

The amount of useful material you extract from this book will be directly related to your level of decomposition. While fresh zombies have always exhibited a higher capacity for learning, in some rare cases, heavily decomposed zombies have managed to retain some knowledge as well.

Finally, please be advised that some contents of this book are graphic in nature, and could make you hungry.

Sincerely,

ZED.

1

WHAT THE HELL AM I?

Zedulations, you're a zombie! You are one of the newest appendages of an alliance of infected ex-humans, a creature seasoned for a single duty: to gorge upon the living. The zombie virus stuffed in your innards borrows the human body—similar to "borrowing a tissue"—shutting off all your wasteful bodily functions then reanimating you with a hunger that defies the laws of human science. Your body is now controlled by roughly 50 billion contaminated neurons in the brain (though, admittedly, we've never counted them), all manipulated to a new purpose: to hunt, fight, and feed.

Prior to your body's metamorphosis, also known as *zombification*, these neurons were highly developed, capable of problem solving, language, memory, and perverted thinking. But once you became infected, all these mental processes were dissolved in a traumatic brain event, even the kinky ones. This viral dementia is precisely the reason you don't remember joining up! Going forward, it will affect your ability to use weapons, hunt cooperatively, and communicate during the pursuit of the living. These attributes have been replaced by screaming, drooling, shambling, and other zed mannerisms, which may or may not come in handy.

Once the z-virus is introduced into a system, it is 100 percent incurable, so rest assured: your position in the Army of Darkness is irrevocable. However, in order to remain a productive member of our team, you must consume and absorb uninfected flesh to decelerate decomposition.

The good news is, you are well equipped with the weapons necessary to gain access to your tasty prey. Your newly transformed brain cells still erratically control all gross motor skills, allowing your zombie body to be clumsily mobile and react to the world in a limited, instinctual way. With the help of newly enhanced zombie senses, these crude motor skills are all you need to track and dine on the living. In addition, you're impervious to pain and capable of absorbing large amounts of damage, including the loss of appendages or major organs. Your body will keep on ticking until it's disconnected from your brain, whether through decapitation, blunt force trauma, fire, or cranial penetration.

It's a lot to absorb, but throughout the rest of the book all the information you need will be regurgitated in body-dragging detail.

Screw Responsibility!

They say infection, we say solution! In your past incarnation, the world was filled with what humans call "responsibilities," grotesque obligations that held you accountable to your peers. But as a zed, you are no longer bedeviled by these rules. In fact, high standards and quality living are actually frowned upon in the zombie world. As the Zombie Code clearly states, "A zombie shall never follow the laws of man, punishable by decapitation" (see "The Zombie Code," page 143). So F responsibilities!

Need specifics? Here are just a few of the human distractions from which the z-virus has freed you.

- **Taxes.** The government may be looking for you, but it's probably not because your 1040 form was late. If they want it, they can come and get it. You could give a rat's ass about W2s when you have WWZ on your tainted mind.

- **Work.** In past lives, most zombies were chained to demeaning desk jobs and tortured by asshole bosses. Consider this an early retirement. The time for pushing pencils and processing numbers is over—this is the time to burn bridges!

- **Investments.** Remember having to save for your financial future? No, you probably don't, and that's for the best. If you'd known that the currency-free existence of a zombie awaited you, you could have just bought that damn sports car!

- **Dieting.** South Beach, North Beach . . . you've counted your last calorie. The Brain Beach Diet is not restrictive.

- **Hygiene.** Body maintenance is now out of your hands, assuming you still have them. Even without a daily grooming routine, you'll still turn heads, trust us. A slow shamble down any main street will have all the girls and boys screaming.

- **Sleep.** Party all night long! Zombies don't need sleep, which allows us to hunt continually, sun up or sun down!

- **Social Networking.** As a human, you probably spent much of your time dodging shady acquaintances and their "friend requests." Now they'll be the ones avoiding you.

- **Dating.** Zeds are not great with relationships; they often mistake attempts at intimacy for an aggressive attack and respond accordingly. Think on the bright side: no more buying flowers or forgetting anniversaries. Good for you, bad for Hallmark.

Zombie History

Like zombies throughout history, you roam in the present by the seat of your soiled pants. You have enough trouble just staggering day to day, and probably don't have any interest in eyeballing your gloomy past. Unfortunately, this fixed mindset can be unhealthy (just like you!). When it comes to sustained destruction, the undead have a mediocre legacy, and without some slight rubbernecking, history can easily repeat itself. We've ripped out most of the blood-soaked details, narrowing it down to a skeletal outline.

Prehistoric Zombies

Zombo sapiens stumbled into West Africa roughly 200,000 years ago, hauntingly close to the time of modern man—*Homo sapiens*. Evidence indicates that in the beginning, breathers and the undead had many similarities. Both species exhibited shoddy communications skills, lacked personal hygiene, and occasionally experimented with cannibalism.

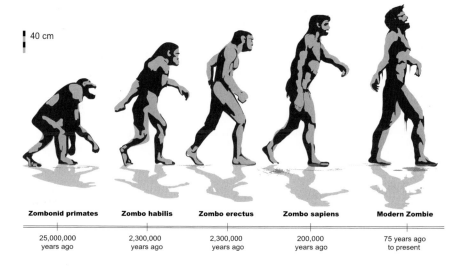

40 cm

Zombonid primates	Zombo habilis	Zombo erectus	Zombo sapiens	Modern Zombie
25,000,000 years ago	2,300,000 years ago	2,300,000 years ago	200,000 years ago	75 years ago to present

The ancient zeds lacked any zombie culture, though they did exhibit primitive communal dynamics, assembling into *hordes*, also known as *mobs* or *zombie walks*, to hunt down their elusive prey. With relatively few humans to feed on, the ancient zeds were often on the brink of severe decomposition. Once massed together, early *Zombo sapiens* would rely heavily on the newly reanimated to sniff out hidden human flesh. If a human victim was located, the new recruits' screams and moans would shatter the stale air and stimulate the starved pack to close in on the bewildered human. Flesh proportions would have to be shared.

Not only was *Zombo sapiens'* existence a constant struggle for survival, but also the ancient strain of the z-virus was weak by today's standards. For both these reasons, our earliest ancestors succeeded in infesting only a minuscule portion of the human population.

Soon, however, populations of *Homo sapiens* and *Zombo sapiens* were both on the rise, and it became more difficult to coexist. Uninfected humans invented stone tools, including blunt weapons, and embraced pointlessly aggressive behavioral patterns. Armed and dangerous, the living were now killing zombies for pleasure, a murderous pursuit that previewed humankind's bloody future.

With an undead genocide underway, the zeds were forced to evolve in order to survive. They developed a persistent hunger for brains that transcended their basic need for nourishment. Other evolutionary adaptations also occurred: increased adrenaline production, and changes in the positioning of the larynx and hyoid bone that improved their projectile vomiting abilities.

The Zombie of Dolni figure is one of the earliest known depictions of the walking undead. Found in the Czech Republic, it has been dated to approximately 28,000 years ago.

With the zeds bullied into aggressiveness, zombie attacks began to rise during the Middle Paleolithic Age, about 150,000 years ago. Our ancestors began to experiment with nocturnal hunting; they could more easily locate breathing humans in the dark, while the defending breathers found it more difficult to see clearly and defend themselves. Soon, with an estimated world population of around 4,000 living and 400 undead, humans were on the brink of extinction. Unfortunately, ancient zombies lacked the ambition to finish the job, a pesky trait many of us suffer from to this day.

The living, on the other hand, took action to ensure their own survival. Around 40,000 B.C., they began to migrate away from zombie-infested territories. Armed with hunting spears and food rations, they divided into three tribes and set off in different directions, thus beginning the exodus from Africa. Hungry and pissed off, the undead straggled behind, feasting on the weak.

The first human tribe set out north, along the Nile River, then navigated into southern Asia. The zombie horde kept pace, shadowing the living, until their sluggish eating habits created an unbridgeable distance between them and their remaining enemies. The humans had outmaneuvered the flesh hunters, and the zombie horde's fate is unrecorded.

The second tribe crossed the Red Sea, which at that time was 230 feet lower than its present level. Once across the strait, the living continued marching east toward the coastal regions of what is now India. Trying to contain the humans, the zombies pushed them to the Beringia land bridge, which connected Asia to present-day North America. Unfortunately, the pursuers were ill prepared to cross the thousand-mile ice-covered tundra; the freezing conditions rendered their undead bodies useless (see "Cold," page 62), and they were ultimately lost to the elements. It is assumed that the humans survived and completed their journey into North America.

It wasn't until the third tribe migrated that we achieve a feasting victory. This last tribe of breathers headed south, not realizing their journey

Exodus Out of Africa
40,000 years ago

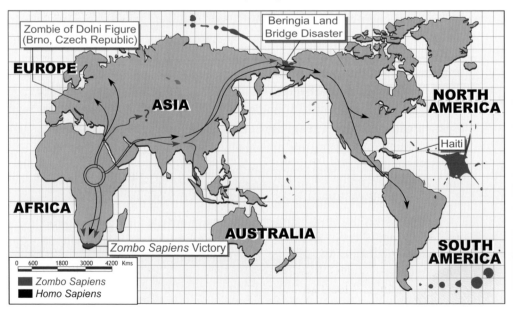

Zombie of Dolni Figure
(Brno, Czech Republic)

Beringia Land
Bridge Disaster

EUROPE

ASIA

NORTH
AMERICA

Haiti

AFRICA

AUSTRALIA

SOUTH
AMERICA

Zombo Sapiens Victory

0   600   1800   3000   4200 Kms

Zombo Sapiens
Homo Sapiens

would come to abrupt stop at the coast. Quickly outnumbered by the pursuing undead (Go, zed, go!), the tribe was overtaken and hunted to extinction.

With these three great migrations, the z-virus was out, spread globally. Further outbreaks could now strike any time, anywhere.

The Zombie Name

The birth of an everlasting name! Although humankind had whispered warnings about the undead menace for thousands of centuries, it wasn't until relatively recently that they granted us recognition in the form of our own name: *zombie*. The term was coined in the 16th century A.D. by a bunch of tasty Central and West African slaves. Kidnapped from Africa by transatlantic slave traders, these displaced tribesmen were soon confronted with a number of hardships waiting in the New World, including our rambunctious company.

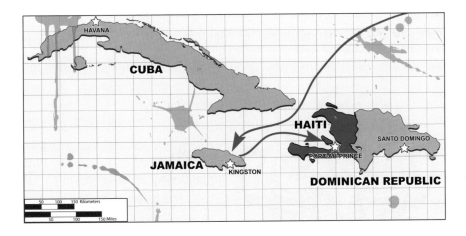

Exhausted from hours in the hot cotton, coffee, and tobacco fields of Haiti, the slaves became easy targets, and our Caribbean ancestors stealthily gobbled them down under cover of darkness. Because the torture of slaves was a regular occurrence, our victims' screams of pain were completely ignored, and our night hunting continued unopposed—until, during one attack, we got a little sloppy.

It appears that a lone slave survived to witness our undead, cannibalistic feeding habits. Our secret was out, and we noticed that slaves began to travel in groups with farm tools as makeshift weapons for protection. These groups were often a mix of West and Central African people who spoke a variety of native languages. Those who spoke Kimbundu, coming out of Angola, called us *nzumbe* or *nzambi*, a word that means "spirit of a dead person." People from the Congo spoke Bantu and called us *zondi*, a word that means "ghost" or "soul of a dead person." It wasn't long before these displaced people combined the words into *zombie* (*ZOM-bee*), which would enter the English lexicon in 1871.

NZUMBE + ZONDI = ZOMBIE

As for the slaveholders, at first they assumed that the tales of undead attackers were just myths, products of the slaves' voodoo religion. They misdiagnosed our killings as animal attacks. But there were no major predators in Haiti (crocodiles and iguanas were quickly exonerated), and of course devoured human carcasses began to turn up, surrounded by our stumbling humanoid footprints. Slave owners eventually decided that the myths must be true—and that voodoo itself was to blame for the attacks. They quickly forbade the public practice of the religion, forced voodoo practitioners to convert to Catholicism, and accused voodoo priests and priestesses of witchcraft, but the attacks did not cease. And the slaves, who knew their religion was not to blame for our eating habits, continued to secretly practice voodoo to preserve their culture. This is why today we are often associated with voodoo.

Of course, even the slaves' understanding of our nature was horribly inaccurate. To suggest that we are merely the spirits of dead humans—it's an insult! It wasn't until the mid-1900s that the breathers fully understood our dreaded behavior and constructed a new, more accurate definition of the term *zombie*: an undead body that feeds on the living. That's us!

Other Zombie Names

Our rotten team has cataloged a more complete list of names the humans have bestowed upon the walking dead.

banshees	mindless drones	stenchers
biters	moaners	stiffs
bloodeaters	mutants	stumblers
boomers	*ndzumbi*	toxic avengers
brain-eaters	*nzambe*	toxic Zs
brainless	*nzumbe*	the undead
the Brainy Bunch	parahumans	the undying
carriers	plague carriers	walkers
chompers	post-lifers	the walking dead
crawlers	the reanimated	walking corpses
creepers	red-eyes	Zacks
the damned	the restless dead	*zambi*
deadheads	the risen	zed-heads
the decomposed	the rising	zeds
decomps	Romero types	zeros
drifters	the rotted	zom-bustibles
the evil dead	rotters	*zombi*
flesh-eaters	revenants	the zombified
ghouls	Satan's soldiers	*Zombo sapiens*
the grave dead	screamers	zombies
greenies	shamblers	Zs
the half-rotten	shufflers	*zumbi*
hulks	shuffling dead	_____*
immolators	*siafu*	_____
the infected	souless body	_____
the living dead	specters	_____
jujus	stenches	_____

The living are constantly coming up with insulting names for us, so scribble additional names you overhear for reference.

The Modern Zombie

Over the last few decades, boneheaded human scientists have inadvertently begun to contribute to the undead cause. At this very moment, they are experimenting with genetically engineered, highly contagious versions of the z-virus. If one of these test-tube strains were accidentally introduced into the general population, it could unleash an unstoppable zombie pandemic, a scenario we've being itching for for centuries.

But we modern zombies can't just lie in wait, hoping that some foolhardy breather will do our job for us. If zed history has taught us anything, it's that we must remain vigilant and lunge at every opportunity that presents itself. The humans continue to evolve—greater weapons, a greater appetite for war and destruction—and so must we. One thing is certain: until the living no longer exist, we cannot rest.

Significant Events in Zed History

200,000 B.C.	The rise of *Zombo sapiens*
40,000 B.C.	Exodus out of Africa, early migration of the undead
22,000 B.C.	Beringia land bridge disaster
9,600 B.C.	Extermination of Atlantis
3,000 B.C.	Battle of Stonehenge
480 B.C.	Battle of Thermopylae
250 B.C.	Crossing of the Great Wall of China
717–718 A.D.	Siege of Constantinople
1340 A.D.	Zombie plague of Europe (a.k.a. the Black Death)
1527 A.D.	War against the Inca Empire
1871 A.D.	Great Chicago Fire (zed and lantern)
1888 A.D.	Takeover of Easter Island
1920 A.D.	Mutation of Creutzfeldt-Jakob disease (a.k.a. mad cow disease)
1925 A.D.	Col. Percy Harrison Fawcett discovers "Lost" City of Z, is eaten
1941–1944 A.D.	Zombie defense of Leningrad
2009 A.D.	Early stages of zed outbreak ("swine flu" epidemic)

Not in the Family

Now that you've been introduced to your undead heritage, you may feel the urge to reach out to the zombie horde. Not so fast—you still have a lot left to learn! First, you must be able to distinguish between fellow zeds who share your destiny, and zedlike humanoids who are not on your side. Remember, a breather's body is vulnerable not only to the z-virus but also to all types of other intruders. Just because it smells like a zombie and looks like a zombie, doesn't mean it *is* a zombie! Study this list to better identify nonzombie types you may encounter during your roaming.

- ☣ **Intoxicated Humans.** During the early stages of a zombie outbreak, humans may attempt to escape the reality of their hopeless situation by overconsuming alcoholic beverages or hallucinogenic drugs. These substances will mimic many symptoms of zombification, including impaired balance, slurred speech, reddened eyes, and impulsive behavior.

  How to Identify Them: They emit puffs of smoke or hold containers of fluid.

  Can You Eat Them? Yes, hiccupping or not. Intoxicated humans are easy prey, as they are often falling asleep or distracted by the munchies. And better still, intoxicated human flesh has a "kick."

- ☣ **The Sick.** Humans constantly battle thousands of nonzombie viruses. These invading organisms can cause fevers, paralysis, comas, and even heart stoppage, all symptoms of zombification. However, none of these viruses cause reanimation. Other symptoms that might confuse you are the stench of decomposing flesh (gangrene), discoloration, and vomiting.

How to Identify Them: Look for hospital beds, thermometers, and IV bags.

Can You Eat Them? Sure! Whatever you have is far worse than what they have.

☣ **The Mentally Disturbed.** Some humans are so overwhelmed by a zombie invasion that they lose all mental control. They begin to act like their zombie opponents and will even bite other uninfected humans. These "quislings" do not suffer from zombification, although they may actually believe they are infected.

How to Identify Them: Mentally disturbed humans smell of fresh flesh and are possibly bound by other humans.

Can You Eat Them? Yes. No matter what the mental capacity of a "Q" victim, brains taste like brains.

☣ **The Demoniacal.** Occasionally, living humans are victims of demonic possession—that is, host to evil spirits that are trying to enter the world of the living using the victim as a gateway. When possessed, the human body is under the partial or full control of the demon and could exhibit zombielike behavior.

How to Identify Them: Excessive cursing (normal) and spinning heads (not normal).

Can You Eat Them? No. Demons are frickin' crazy and unpredictable. Avoid food laced with demonic spirits.

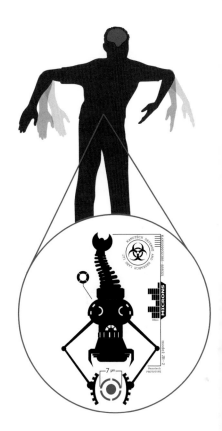

❧ **The Nanoinfected.** Scientists may deliberately introduce microscopic robots into a human body, to either provide the body with physical enhancements (speed and strength, not bosoms) or reprogram it with a new set of objectives. Advanced nanobots may even keep the host body functioning after death, while they search for a new, healthy host and try to transfer themselves via a bite just like the z-virus.

How to Identify Them: While the movements of a fellow zed are jerky and erratic, nanoinfected bodies move with robotic precision. They may also speak, and have a tendency to use repetitive vocabulary.

Can You Eat Them? It's unlikely that nanobots would be programmed to both infiltrate living bodies and kill the undead, so eat up.

❧ **Pretend Zombies.** No, we are not joking. Humans have been observed deliberately mimicking our movements in order to escape or relocate from shoddy hiding places. Oooh, *scary!*

How to Identify Them: Often pretenders try to mask the sweet smell of their flesh with lotions, deodorants, and other smells, but the zombie nose always knows.

Can You Eat Them? Absolutely! These zombie poseurs should be eaten— slowly and alive!

However, if you happen to come within biting distance of a zombie poseur, give the act a few seconds before you begin chomping. Chances are, eager onlookers are waiting to see the results of the strategy before they attempt to escape as well. Be patient and maybe other lemmings will follow.

2

YOUR ZOMBIE BODY

No need to ask your doctor if the z-virus is right for you—a zombified body is a definite upgrade from your fragile human form. As a human, you were vulnerable to freak accidents, countless fatal diseases, and cheeseburger-induced heart attacks. Strange as it seems, the deadly virus may have actu-ally *prolonged* your stay on earth. If in fact, if you were scheduled for a toe tag, the z-virus may have been your winning lottery ticket. So go on, make the most of your new body like you stole it—because you did! This chapter will show you how.

Body Parts of Importance

In your oxygen-rich past, your human body was a veritable smorgasbord of complex parts, each dedicated to a unique function necessary for the operation of the whole. Sounds interesting, right?

Wrong! This overly complicated system serves no purpose in the undead universe. The z-virus took the opportunity to trash-can most of its functions, and those that remain have been altered almost beyond recognition. However, after the elegant artistry of the zombification process, the leftovers are surprisingly efficient. You may even say *superior*. From flesh to claws, the zombie body is fully equipped to serve as an instrument of human destruction.

For example, the virus has modified the muscles in your jaw, relaxing and elongating them to increase your chewing force—quite beneficial when chomping human flesh. In addition, your jaw has become more flexible, making it possible to literally fit your foot in your mouth—or someone else's. The modifications also increase your swallowing potential.

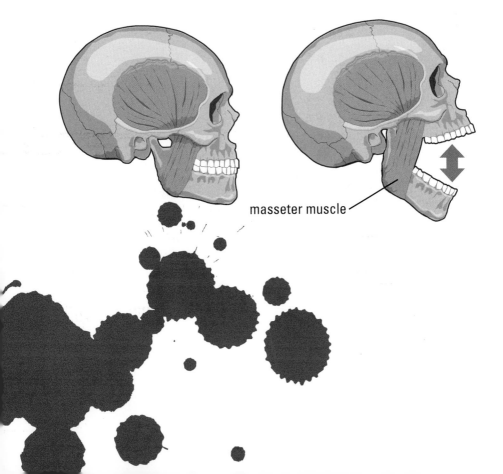

masseter muscle

Scan the menu below for more juicy facts on your most important zed equipment.

- **Arms.** Your arm bone should be connected to your hand bone, and your hand bone catches food. Zeds blessed with two arms have a higher success rate when hunting. Some quick-witted zombies are also capable of using their hands for holding weapons or operating simple human mechanisms. Some rare strains of the z-virus will allow a zombie's arms to remain active even after they've been disconnected from its body; this type of motion is known as *zedothermic movement*.

HEAD

ARM

- **Legs.** Are you a leg guy or gal—meaning, do you have two of them? These helpful appendages are responsible for moving you from one place to another. Decomposition and other viral side effects have likely hampered their coordination, which is why you have that stereotypical zombie limp, shuffle, or shamble. Legs on fresh zeds move the fastest, so use them before you lose them! Newly undead zombies are capable of adrenaline bursts that surpass those of the average zed, allowing them to move at incredible speeds of up to one step every 1.5 seconds.

LEG

- **Head.** Hey, zed head, without your melon, your body wouldn't work. It's packed with the precious infected brain matter that drives you. If your cranium experiences trauma, termination is probable, so be cautious! Just as important, your moan machine—the mouth—is the entry point for human flesh. Most heads are also graced with eyes, ears, and a nose. Lucky for you, the z-virus has enhanced these organs to aid in hunting and combat; see the next section for more details.

Use Your Head!

Zombies aren't known for using their heads, but a zed noggin is actually a useful tool for registering stimuli during a human hunt. The z-virus infuses a zombie's eyes, ears, and nose with extraordinary sensory abilities. By honing your enhanced sight, smell, and hearing and coordinating with other members of the horde (see "Body Language," page 25), you can pinpoint the location of even the craftiest breather.

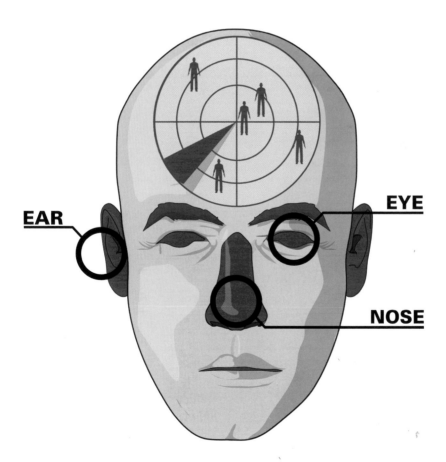

EAR

EYE

NOSE

Eyes

Your rotten eyes don't lie—there is no question your eyeballs are different from a human's. Your eyes' light receptors changed during zombification; while the cells responsible for detecting bright light remained virtually untouched, those responsible for working in low light, detecting motion, and providing basic visual information have become highly specialized. Consequently, what appears to be pitch black to a breather is still dimly lit to a zed.

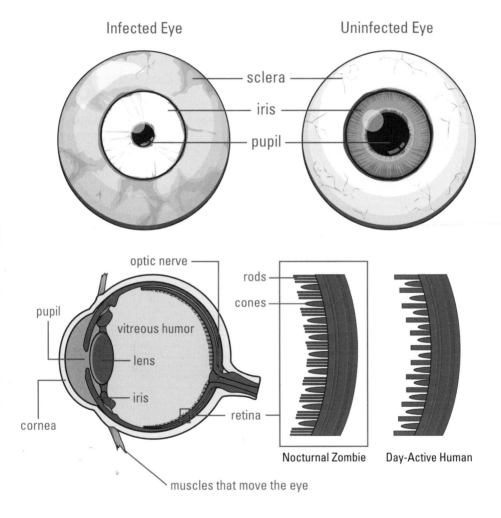

Infected Eye   Uninfected Eye

sclera
iris
pupil

optic nerve
pupil
vitreous humor
lens
iris
cornea
rods
cones
retina
muscles that move the eye

Nocturnal Zombie   Day-Active Human

Besides amplifying light for hunting prey under the cover of darkness, your zombie eyes also provide you with improved peripheral vision. This is not the result of your modified light receptors but the side effect of dehydration, which has caused your eyeball to shorten. This shortening causes light rays to focus behind the retina. As a result, your eyes now see distant objects more clearly, while anything within a few inches of you is blurred. Unfortunately, this farsightedness affects all zeds when defending and attacking at close range.

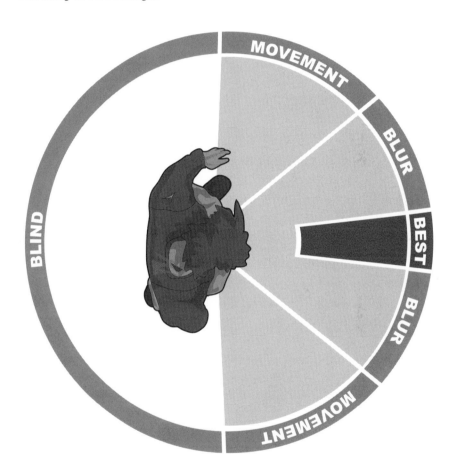

Through a combination of these changes, you may also experience an increase in remote vision. This will allow you to detect the smooth body motion of an uninfected human out of range of your other senses.

What condition are your eyes in? Review the Zombie Eye Chart on the next page. The silhouettes on the top two lines—military, firefighters, police, ninjas, martial art experts, Chuck Norris, and loggers with chainsaws—should be avoided. On the next two lines are other humans who *should* be targeted—either because they are generally weaker or because their special skills could benefit the human resistance: the elderly and injured, children, medical staff, white-collar office workers, clowns, and farmers (humans need food, right?).

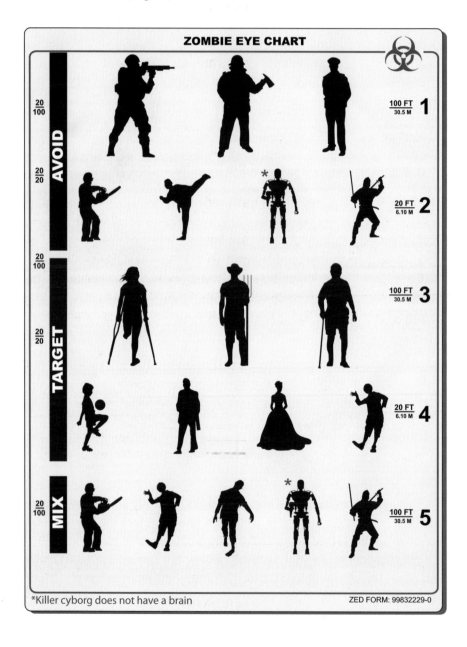

ZOMBIE EYE CHART

*Killer cyborg does not have a brain

ZED FORM: 99832229-0

Of course, before the outbreak is over, even the trickier targets will have to be dealt with. But all their brains taste the same, so why not start with those who will put up less of a fight?

Ears

Don't be alarmed that you cannot see your ears. They're there, right on the sides of your head. Before reanimation, they were responsible for assessing the stupidity of other uninfected humans. The z-virus determined that prejudging others was not necessary in your post-life, so now your ears can only detect the basic sounds made by the living, not evaluate them.

> ## "The ear of the zombie must ring with the voices of the living."
> ## —ZEDROW WILSON, 1800s

Test results have shown that fresh zeds share the same auditory range as a human. In addition, though all humans have the biological capability to wiggle their ears, most breathers have not developed this talent. But here's a surprise—drumroll, please—almost all zombies can! When you were zombified, the virus activated the underdeveloped muscles attached to your ears that make this shifting possible. Once stimulated, your ears are now capable of slight motion that can help determine the direction of noises.

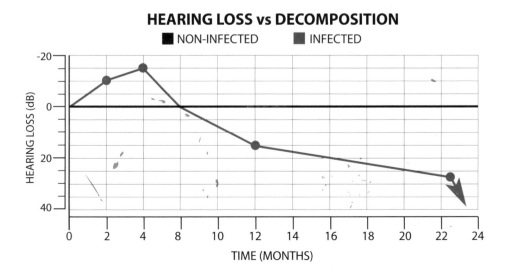

HEARING LOSS vs DECOMPOSITION
NON-INFECTED   INFECTED

HEARING LOSS (dB)

TIME (MONTHS)

However, you may lose all hearing ability during later stages of post-life. Eventually your ear canals (external auditory canals) will clog with decomposing tissue, blocking the inner ears' ability to function. In addition, you may experience an increasing problem maintaining your balance. Hearing impairment from decomposition in the ear canals can sometime be cured with a quick dip in water, but damage to the inner ear cannot be undone.

Nose

On a hunt, your nose can capture the sweet fragrance of human flesh. Cleverly located between your eyes, but slightly lower, your zed sniffer is capable of not only smelling living prey up to a mile away but also determining its direction. This can be more difficult in an urban environment; the abundance of odors is sometimes overwhelming.

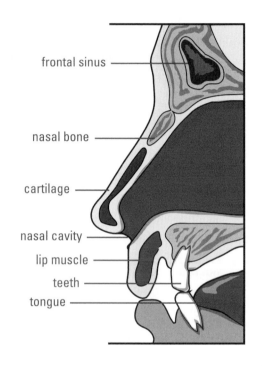

frontal sinus

nasal bone

cartilage

nasal cavity

lip muscle

teeth

tongue

During decomposition, your nose fills with low levels of toxic mucus. When the living prey's pheromones—found in their blood, sweat, and other secretions—come in contact with this mucus, your nose instantly registers it and triggers adrenaline-like neurotransmitters in your brain. Which direction your prey is located is then determined by which nasal receptors detect a change in contact levels. When the prey's direction is pinpointed, you're off and shambling toward it. (Sounds advanced, doesn't it?)

Excessive snot may seep into your mouth—which can

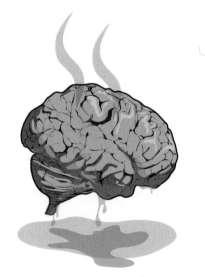

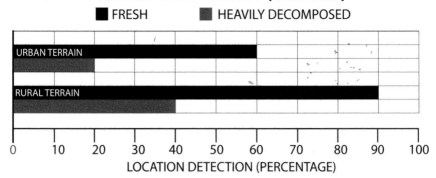

SMELLING EFFICIENCY (TERRAIN)

■ FRESH   ■ HEAVILY DECOMPOSED

URBAN TERRAIN									
RURAL TERRAIN									

| 0 | 10 | 20 | 30 | 40 | 50 | 60 | 70 | 80 | 90 | 100 |

LOCATION DETECTION (PERCENTAGE)

lead to projectile vomiting, since your body will reject consuming anything other than flesh. Your nose will also experience bleeding after a full meal.

Sensory Deprivation

Unfortunately, the humanoid body (living or zed) is equipped with only two eyes, two ears, and one nose. Most zeds eventually lose one or more of these organs through clumsiness, human resistance, or severe decomposition. ("Everyone freeze—my eyeball just popped out!") Don't be alarmed if you are missing one of your senses; you can still call on the senses of other zombies through communal hunting. By mobbing together, you not only increase your physical strength but also join up with recently reanimated, fresh zeds who are capable of locating humans more than a mile away.

If attacking with a horde is impossible, sense-deprived zombies should consider "hide and wait" hunting techniques (see "Waiting for Food," page 48).

Body Language

Article VIII of the Zombie Code strictly prohibits zombies from attempting to engage in coherent speech, under penalty of tongue removal (see "The Zombie Code," page 143). But are zombies even capable of talking? Verbal communication is very rare for a zed, because the z-virus damages the auditory center of the brain. If speech is possible, it's usually slurred gibberish. Ever hear the phrase "Spray it, don't say it"? Zombies coined that! Most of us are limited to moaning or screaming when alerted to danger or potential prey. Sorry to knock you off your pedestal, but most predatory animals use the same techniques to rally or warn their fellow hunters—including the brainy breathers.

In situations that require more precise communication, your best bet is to resort to nonverbal techniques—flirtatious gestures, facial expressions, etc. Swinging your hips or turning your head in the direction of your quarry will send a directional message rippling through the horde.

What's Your Body Type?

Don't worry, this isn't a quiz! The undead come in all shapes and sizes, but whether dismembered or appendage-privileged, each zombie body can be stuffed into one of three basic categories. Once you determine your body type, exploit your strengths and avoid your weaknesses.

☣ **Ectomorph (Bony):** An ectomorph is a small and fragile zed with narrow shoulders and hips. Its body is lightly muscled but flexible, with a longer stride, and it is capable of unusual speeds (a.k.a. banshee speeds). Ectomorphs should eat human flesh frequently but in small amounts.

   Ideal Horde Duties: Tracking and hunting human flesh.

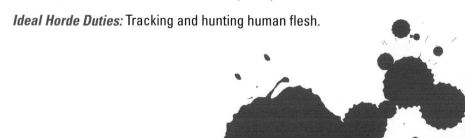

⚕ **Mesomorph (Shambler).** This zed is considered lean and muscular, at least for a decomposing body. Its shoulders are usually wider than its hips, and it is typically stronger than zombies of the other two body types. However, mesomorphs have a tendency to overdo it, and often suffer muscle damage as a result.

Ideal Horde Duties: Barricade smashing or human extraction.

⚕ **Endomorph (Boomer).** An endomorph's shape resembles an apple or pear, with a larger bottom than top. Sometimes called a *hulk*, it is both curvy and overweight, less agile, and sometimes slower than zombies of the other two body types. Endomorphs should monitor flesh consumption, as they have a higher risk of gastric explosion. Larger bodies also make larger targets. Tight squeezes can be problematic.

Ideal Horde Duties: Bullet shielding and toxic landmine laying.

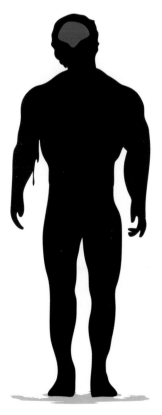
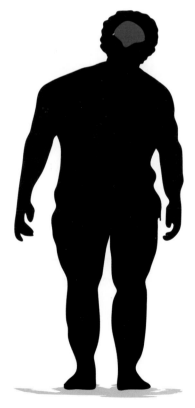

Ectomorph   Mesomorph   Endomorph

Post-life Expectancy

Unfortunately, reanimated bodies don't shamble forever. How long you last depends on two things: the current condition of your corpse and your monthly flesh diet. Ultimately, natural decay will eat away at your body, eventually rendering your corpse incapable of movement before you finally dissolve into nothingness. Zombies take longer to decay than conventional cadavers, because the potent z-virus fends off bacteria and other organisms that cause decomposition. However, if you neglect to nourish the virus by feeding on uninfected flesh, you will disintegrate at a more traditional rate; a starving zombie's "shamble span" is estimated at four to nine months. (Your results may vary.) On the other hand, if you regularly feed on the living to maintain your decomposing body (see "Human Buffet," page 105), you could last for two years or more.

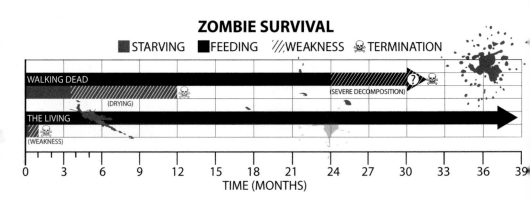

Body Q&A

Many flesh-craving zeds are quick to join the hunt before asking themselves some very important questions. We've picked the brains of fellow zombies and documented the most-moaned questions.

Q: Do I need air?

A: No. While a living human can only live approximately six minutes without air, a zombie is entirely oxygen independent. Its respiratory system, whether damaged or intact, is obsolete. Zeds can even survive in aquatic environments without risk of drowning, though prolonged exposure to water can increase decomposition. Of course, this also means you are safe from suffocation.

Q: Am I vulnerable to anything?

A: Yes: brain damage by cranial penetration, brain stem trauma, or decapitation will stop you in your tracks. If your head is damaged by fire, this can also lead to termination, though your complete cremation could take up to 40 minutes (see "The Flame," page 92).

Q: Am I allergic to anything?

A: Yes. Human bodies that have been dead longer than 12 hours should not be consumed. This tainted flesh has no nutritional value and may cause stomach buildup and absorption blocking. Improper feeding can lead to blindness and other complications. Toe tags are a good indicator that your meal is spoiled.

Q: Do controlled substances affect me?

A: Most drugs, poisons, and gases have no effect on you, though under rare circumstances, intoxicated humans can cause disorientation (see "Intoxicated Humans," page 11). You should avoid acid, which can quickly dissolve the flesh it contacts, though acid damage is generally highly localized.

Q: Did the z-virus heal my human impairments?

A: Possibly, depending on the damage. The virus will not regenerate missing body parts, but it does form new intercellular connections to reanimate your undead corpse. On rare occasions these connections will reactivate previously nonfunctional organs, curing blindness, deafness, or other infirmities left over from your human years.

3

KNOW YOUR ENEMY

Who is your enemy?

Simply put, your enemy is a warm body containing an uninfected human brain. The world is filled with more than 6 billion of them—that's an astounding 135 million tons of gray matter, or 10.3 million fully loaded dump trucks! Unfortunately, humans refuse to simply load their brains into dump trucks for us to consume. Instead, even in the midst of a full-blown zombie outbreak, the breathers' inquiring minds will continue to focus on their own selfish needs. In order to hunt them successfully, you'll need to understand what those needs are and how they influence the behavior of your prey.

Human Needs

Breathers are quite capable of pigging out, just like you. A zed once witnessed a single human downing 80 chicken nuggets in five minutes. And while this is abnormal, a healthy mortal will need to digest roughly 2,500 calories of food a day—about 40 chicken nuggets—to maintain their fragile biological processes. That's approximately 1.2 pounds of chow, about one-third the weight of an average adult human brain. Along with fast food, they also need water, shelter, and alcohol. These are the bare essentials a human requires to live long and prosper.

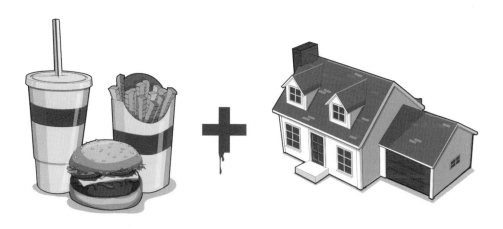

But then some old guy named Maslow made a real mess of things by beefing up this list with a few "emotional" needs. They include a sense of belonging, self-esteem, and self-actualization, whatever the hell that is. And while friendship and respect are not essential for our survival, according to Maslow they are a must for humanity.

This baffling array of needs will eventually affect the sanity of all last-ditch defenders of the living. As they yearn for respect, friendship, or sexual intimacy—our money is on intimacy—they will neglect their more basic needs and their personal safety. By understanding this tendency, we can exploit humans' weaknesses. The following insights expose how vulnerable the living truly are, not knowing that at any moment their civilization hangs by a vein.

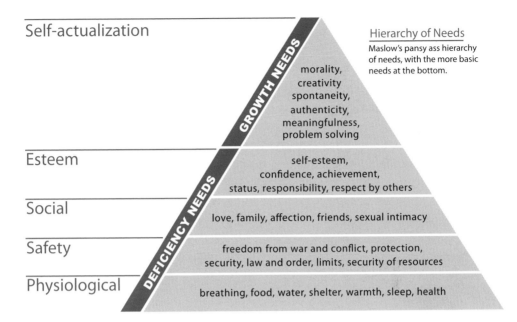

Self-actualization

Esteem

Social

Safety

Physiological

GROWTH NEEDS

DEFICIENCY NEEDS

morality, creativity spontaneity, authenticity, meaningfulness, problem solving

self-esteem, confidence, achievement, status, responsibility, respect by others

love, family, affection, friends, sexual intimacy

freedom from war and conflict, protection, security, law and order, limits, security of resources

breathing, food, water, shelter, warmth, sleep, health

Hierarchy of Needs
Maslow's pansy ass hierarchy of needs, with the more basic needs at the bottom.

Humans Will Make Mistakes

During past crises, both natural and zombie-made, humans have made costly miscalculations or become disoriented to the point of uselessness. The next zombie plague will be no different. Both physical and emotional needs will hamper their decision making and increase your feeding opportunities. What follows are some major mistakes your prey will likely make.

Poorly Prepared

Most humans approach the likelihood of a zed epidemic the same way they approach the possibility of a huge asteroid hitting the earth: they assume it just isn't going to happen. Tell that to what became the Gulf of Mexico 60 million years ago! Even after reports of the walking dead start coming in, some humans will assume it's a media hoax, not unlike the alien attack panic caused by Orson Welles in 1938. (Aliens? Yeah, right!)

This skepticism has crippled their preparedness. As we've moaned before, humans need an ample amount of provisions to survive. They are very capable of this task; their homes are stockpiled with enough pornography to outlast an outbreak, but they can't eat porn. In a single year, a human will need about 430 pounds of food and 170 pounds of water . . . or 91 cases of beer. Except for screwball survivalists, how many humans do you think actually have this much stockpiled today? The answer is very few. No wonder humans cut and run once the party runs out of chips and salsa.

Crawling out of their protective shelters, humans will be drawn to places such as Super Food City and Doug's Donut World to find anything edible. Desperation can also lead to violence among remaining survivors; they might attack each other over Twinkies and Spam. These scenarios can produce wounded or hungry humans, slow-moving zombie food that you can quickly gobble up.

However, do not assume that *all* mortals will be unprepared for a zombie uprising. Zed groupies and other secret "zombie awareness" groups are ready. However, none of these brainy bands have amassed numbers large enough to hinder a ziege.

Insufficiently Protected Against Infection

"Bless you!" is just a polite way to say, "Thanks for the z-virus!" Most breathers are sneezers who do not take necessary precautions during a viral outbreak. Mouths, noses, eyes, and wounds should all be covered, but they won't be. Their careless behavior is our opportunity to recruit new members to our undead team (see "Infecting," page 117).

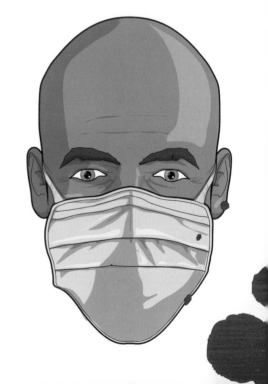

Humans who are already infected but who have not yet succumbed to death and reanimation will further our causes by continuing to interact with the general public. Some will use public transportation as they search for a cure or try to find family. While it's pure carelessness on the part of the breathers, we welcome their assistance.

Terrible with Weapons

According to our undead sources, the human race hasn't yet cloned Chuck Norris. (Phew!) Even luckier for us, only a small percentage of the living have even been trained to be mercenaries. Yes, weapon possession is high, but they mostly consist of cutlery knives and nontraceable handguns— "miniweapons," you might say. Scrambling for protection, humans might use anything, from clubbed weapons to simple wooden boards.

Unless they land a lucky blow to your head, most of these weapons will have no effect on your pain-impervious body. What's more, such weapons require the attacker to be in close proximity, making them easy targets for vomit (see "Projectile Vomiting," page 82). And many improvised weapons cause extensive blood splatter, increasing the risk of infection.

Even gun-toting humans are a manageable threat, as most of them have terrible aim. And as battles rage on, there will be an ammunition shortage; bullets will run out quickly. If you stay to the rear of an attacking horde, you can reduce the risk of a fatal head shot (see "Avoiding the Bullet," page 84).

Physically Not Fit

Human obesity levels are grossly underestimated; the majority of humans are not built for combat. These "biggest losers" have two options: fight or flee. Most jelly bellies choose to avoid pudgy-hand-to-zombie-hand combat, and flee. They can exhibit impressive feats of speed on their oversized legs, but eventually the Big Macs take their toll, causing fatigue and excruciating sideaches.

In the end, the brain-eating turtle wins the race. A persistent zed will exhaust them, though the hunter may face the unpleasant possibility of having to watch these humans blow chunks. If that doesn't make you sick, take a look at the human food below.

Predisposed to Insanity

Breathers are crazy. Their personal feelings can erupt in all sorts of hysterical ways, inevitably decreasing their chances of survival. At the slightest suggestion that they might end up on our menu, humans will panic. They'll randomly wave swords or shoot aimlessly, slashing fellow defenders' jugulars or worse. In addition, claustrophobia, video game withdrawal, or a misguided urge to reunite with family and pets can lead to an ill-advised journey out of a hiding place. Most of this craziness adds up to an easy meal for you.

By the end of a truly devastating zombie outbreak, the breathers may have succumbed to total desperation. They may take their own lives to avoid joining the ranks of the undead—or they may try to join our ranks even without being infected (see "The Mentally Disturbed," page 12).

Always Drawing Attention to Themselves

Hey, look at me, I'm at Pacific Playland! Humans continually evolve and have, just recently, mutated into multitaskers. Case studies have shown that the living today are incapable of sitting quietly. They constantly create noises by humming, tapping, whistling, and talking. These annoying noises piss us off—and tip us off that dinner is served!

Zeds have also observed that the living find it necessary to surround themselves with objects that increase their visibility. Barking dogs, vehicles, weapons, electrical appliances, and other technologies flash before our eyes and ring in our ears, helping us pinpoint which direction we should shamble. When humans shoot out a window, turn on the lights, or let the family dog bark, they're letting you know that you'll be eating good.

At the Mercy of Big Brother

If it's anything like the TV show *Big Brother*, the human resistance is going to be a train wreck! There is no question that during a z-virus epidemic, military personnel or other government officials will be dispatched to "assist" the living. However, this aid will take the form of containment only—officials will simply set up a large perimeter around the infected area.

At this point, it's open season on everyone trapped inside the confines of zombieland. Humans barricaded in homes or other shelters are just leftovers for us to claim. Eventually we'll infect or eat everyone within the perimeter, swell our numbers, and prepare to assault the humans' main line of defense.

There Is No "I" in Human

Unlike the efficient, self-motivated zed, panicked humans need someone to slap them around and tell them what to do. This freakish weakness soon becomes a burden. It starts with complaining, then leads to questioning leadership. Eventually it escalates into something uglier: a once-powerful breather band can be torn apart by irreconcilable differences, making it vulnerable to a zombie horde's attack. Not unlike a severed appendage flailing on the ground, a separated individual becomes an easy target.

Not to toot our own horns, but there *is* an "I" in zombie!

How to Kill a Human

Yes, the living can experience minor injures—muscle soreness, sprains, contusions, tendinitis, and possible fractures—but none of them will guarantee you a brainy dessert. If you scratch or bite a human, they will be infected by the z-virus and will eventually die and join our cause—but you want to eat, dammit! What you need to do is *kill* a human, not just *harm* it. Knock it cold to the ground, then chow down until your face is painted red.

Fortunately, if you can harm it, you can kill it! Breathers come in all shapes and sizes, but absent weapons or protective clothing, bodies of every type are equally susceptible to infection and/or death. Don't be fooled—tattoos will *not* improve your prey's defenses against the horde.

Every human's soft underbelly shares the exact same set of innards: 11 entangled body systems that must continually perform their respective duties to maintain life. If any one system is seriously damaged, the body as a whole cannot function. This interdependency provides you with 1,001 termination possibilities. For example, the human circulatory system is responsible for pumping six quarts of fresh, uninfected blood through thousands of miles of veins. If interrupted, the human goes down, blood squirting everywhere.

Getting hungry yet?

The human body is covered with vulnerable entry points into one or more organ systems. The following slaughter strategies will help you find them. Each one, when executed correctly, will result in something horrible. For them, that is.

Head Trauma

Be a trauma momma and go for the head!

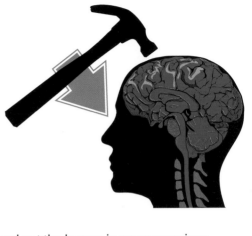

Biting or scratching a breather's facial features can cause major disorientation, and possibly impair your victims' vision (see "Use Your Body as a Weapon," page 81). Without sight, he or she will definitely be at a disadvantage.

You can also use your flailing arms to rain heavy blows to your victim's head. This can bruise its brain and put the human in an unconscious state. Other common symptoms of a bruised brain are dizziness, stroke, seizures, vomiting, aneurysms, nosebleeds, and seeing stars and little birdies.

If pushed to the ground, a human could experience a skull fracture, and a skull fragment could "dent" into the brain. This could lead to quick death, or at least impair your victim while you feast.

And no, battering a brain it does not affect its nutritional value.

Internal Organ Damage

Like a turducken, the human body is stuffed with all types of internal organs. While the human skeleton is highly resistant to damage and human skin is highly resilient, damage done to internal organs such as the liver, kidney, or heart is often delightfully deadly.

To gain access to these organs, concentrate your bites and claws in body locations that offer the least resistance. The diagram on the right shows areas that are not protected by the skeletal system. Use your jaws or claws to break through the skin and tear away until you've damaged something important.

Bleeding

Make them bleed! Many humans go queasy at the sight of blood, and can quickly turn hysterical when they see blood flowing directly out of them.

Fragile humans are also super-duper blood dependent, and will go into shock if they lose even 30–40 percent of the red stuff, guaranteeing you a quiet meal. How can you, a scatterbrained zed, estimate the percentage you've drained? When your unwilling patient turns ghostly white and his or her heartbeat increases, you're on the right track. To increase lethality, aim for a major artery shown on the diagram below.

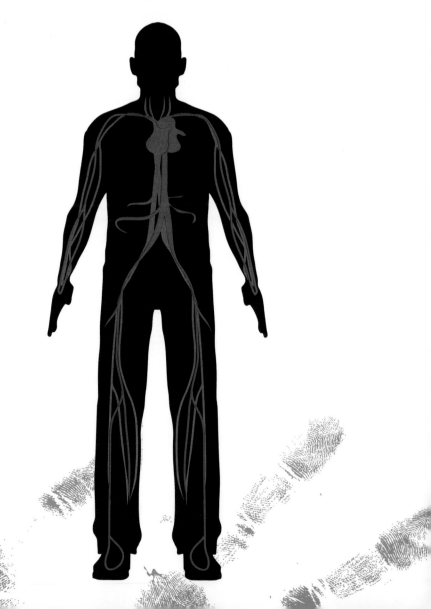

4

HUNTING FOR BRAINS

Can we speak zed-to-zed? You can't keep putting the brain on a pedestal. Uninfected breathers try to brainwash gullible zeds into believing a coherent brain is godlike and unattainable. And though functioning gray matter can be cunning and crafty, it's basically gooey mush.

Brains are also plentiful, though they don't grow on trees. You have to get up off your bony butt and find them! Brain acquisition is the first rite of passage for any new recruit. But locating a human volunteer for your undead hazing is not easy. As all zombies know, heads are attached to bodies, and bodies have legs. A human's are responsible for both locomotion and "consumption prevention"—anything to stay off the menu. Humans will run and hide, which can make obtaining their brains very difficult.

Yet not all humans will be hard to sink your teeth into. During the early stages of any zombie plague, less intelligent humans will be completely oblivious to the severity of the problem and continue to stumble around. As natural selection runs its course, other humans will wise up and get the hell out of sight. When this happens, you will need to develop your unique zombie talents to sniff out the living.

This chapter should assist any zed in the relentless pursuit of living *Homo sapiens*. It will outline successful hunting techniques and provide helpful strategies to penetrate human structures and overcome the obstacles you will face on the hunt.

But be cautious. While there is nothing like the pursuit of a living man, it's only the first step in the feeding process. If you track down a meal only to find yourself unprepared to kill it, you'll not only embarrass yourself but also put yourself in danger. To increase the chances of a successful hunt, carefully study the chapter on combat techniques before setting out (see "Attacking," page 79).

In addition, hunting should always be attempted with fellow zeds. Most hunters are more effective as a pack—or in your case a horde. By communally descending on a single target, it will be more difficult for a swift-moving human to slip though your grasp.

Lunch, Dinner, or Midnight Snack?

Humans are generally more active during daylight and sleep at night to restore their bodies, which makes nighttime the ideal time for a zombie hunt. Most humans will be unprepared or resting, which makes them easy targets. In many cases, humans snore. A snoring human continually makes noises while sleeping, a sound that you can easily detect. Once you spot a group of sleeping humans, target the closest prey; the others will probably awake after you attack.

Once a zombie outbreak is in full swing, however, humans will dramatically alter their daily routine. You will experience human activity at all hours, including the dead of night. Humans often use the cover of darkness to migrate or forage for supplies. Their flashlights, torches, and lanterns are easily visible, even several miles away, depending on weather and terrain. More cautious humans may use the darkness to their advantage, shutting off their lights to conceal their presence. However, this will reduce their own ability to see, increasing these heavy breathers' vulnerability to sneak attacks.

So should you discontinue day hunting? The short answer is no! Even though nocturnal hunting has many advantages, the bright light of day provides amazing visibility. However, some z-virus strains cause extreme light sensitivity, which forces the unlucky zed to hide during daylight and avoid blinding lightbulbs. Photosensitive zombies may also experience severe headaches, made all the worse when accompanied by human screaming.

Tracking

When it comes to hunting, zombies are inherently good trackers, so don't disappoint the horde! With a combination of your specialized senses and an understanding of clues left by the living, it is easy to locate possible human habitations. Here are the most important clues that will help you close in on your meal.

- ☣ **Smoke.** Smoke is a sure sign that something has gone down! While large plumes are usually the result of a car crash or house fire, small wisps of smoke suggest a human settlement. Humans may huddle around a fire to keep warm, and they have the disgusting habit of cooking food over open flames.

- ☣ **Trash.** Humans are megaconsumers—they generate large amounts of trash, and often leave a trail of it behind them. Just follow the shiny candy-bar wrappers and empty bottles and cans, and you should find some unfortunate slob.

- 🦠 **Fortified Structures.** Homes or other buildings that have been fortified against zombie attack—with boarded up windows, for example—are usually stockpiled with brains. (See "Human Structures," page 51.)

- 🦠 **Vehicles.** Cars and trucks that look to be in working condition, especially with abundant supplies strapped to the roof, are a sign that some human is prepared and on the move. (See "Transportation," page 65.)

- 🦠 **Pets.** Breathers love companionship, and where a well-cared-for domestic animal is present, humans are never far behind. Dogs will detect your odor and start barking, which can help you find their owners. In a pinch, pets are suitable for eating (see "Ordering Off the Menu," page 114).

- 🦠 **Noise.** Our advice to you: investigate all noises. Most sounds are the direct result of something man-made or other zeds on the hunt.

Hunting Techniques

Once you've tracked down a promising supply, it's time to round up some humans!

While you might be tempted to make it up as you go, here are a few techniques zeds have developed during past hunts that tend to yield a higher kill rate. Always remember: Safety in numbers and avoid being in front. And do not engage a human before reading the chapter on attack strategies (see page 79).

Baiting

To bait your prey, first immobilize a human decoy, preferably an attractive female. Keep your bait in a state of consciousness; your damsel in distress should remain screaming. In time, concern and arousal will lure other breathers out of hiding to assist her. Their stupidity will be your reward—converge on the human heroes and attack. If they call your bluff and abandon her, just finish her off.

One warning: you may find that zombies outside of your horde will try to steal your bait for their meal. Be prepared for zed-on-zed violence.

Brain Driving

Humans can be success-
fully herded in both rural and
urban settings. The most
difficult part of this tactic is
separating your horde into
two separate stalking groups.
Once that is accomplished,
the first group (the "drivers")
should slowly shamble forward, moaning and scream-
ing. This undead commotion
will alarm the living, who
will flee from the impend-
ing assault—right into a trap
set by your second group of
brain-eaters.

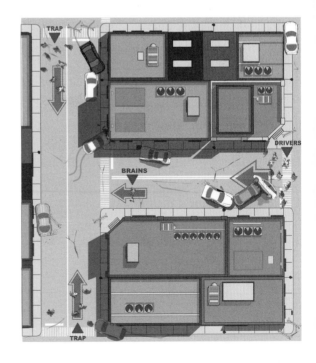

Flesh Flushing

Instinctively, zeds have always relied on flushing techniques, the art of scaring the living out of hiding because of the fear of being eaten alive. This hunting method can create a mass exodus of breathers, right into the flailing arms of the horde outside.

While it might seem straightforward, success is not inevitable. It is very possible that a weapon-welding human is prepared for the initial assault, ready to chop off the head of any invading zombie. Sure, zombies fear nothing, but losing one's head can ruin anyone's day, so avoid being the "flusher" and stick with the waiting horde.

Persistence Hunting

Use your inherent tirelessness to pursue the living to exhaustion. Most human are easily capable of out running an average zombie . . . in the short run. But eventually your prey will need to rest—it's human nature—giving you the opportunity for a burden-free meal.

In this race, slow and steady always wins. If you are missing your legs, try crawling.

ENDURANCE CHART

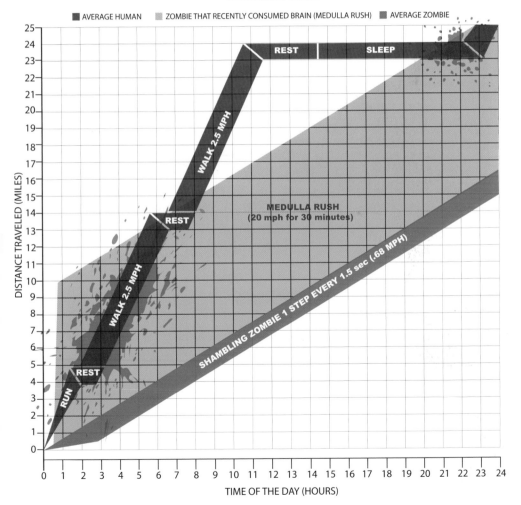

Waiting for Food

When severe decomposition starts affecting your performance, or you've experienced the loss of major appendages, your quest for brains could become wearisome. In order to put food in your mouth, you will need to employ new hunting strategies. While most zombies roam far and wide for food, the patient zombie, hiding in secret, can be just as effective. Eventually, all brains come to those who wait.

The elements of surprise and fear work in your favor when ambushing your quarry. Here are the top 10 places to hide and hunt.

1. **Closet.** General storage areas, from wardrobes to kitchen cabinets, can be found in any human residence. They're perfect for waiting until someone comes home, or a biohazard cleanup crew sweeps through.

2. **Bathroom.** *¿Donde esta el baño?* The bathroom is usually a small enclosed space with few windows, making quick exits difficult. Since every human will eventually need to "use the facilities," catching a human with his or her pants down can make for an easy meal.

3. **Under the Bed.** Yes, the old "monster under the bed" trick! Conceal yourself under or behind furniture, perfect for staying out of sight, out of mind. Wait for your victim's pudgy ankles to walk by, then bite, claw, or grab.

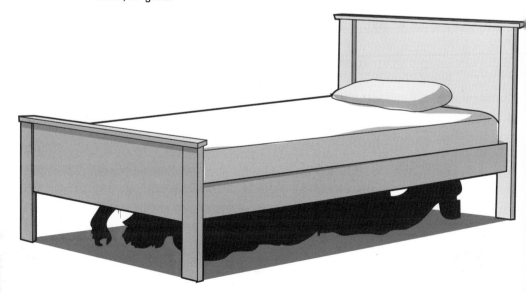

4. **Basement**. With minimal lighting and ample room to maneuver, the cellar is the perfect place to hang out until some human comes down looking for more AA batteries. Zed experience has shown that positioning yourself under the steps can be very successful.

5. **Vehicles**. Operating a car door latch may be above your IQ level, but perhaps someone in your horde will possess the necessary dexterity. Once you gain access to the vehicle, head for the rear. The trunk or backseat is a perfect location to hide until your victim buckles up!

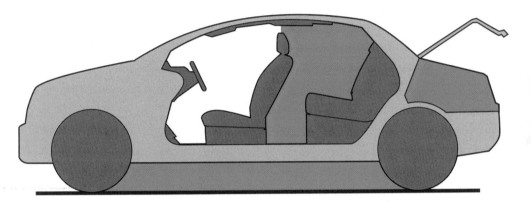

6. **Trash Cans**. A trash can, dumpster, or pile of trash is the perfect cover, though the smell might hamper your ability to detect prey. At the same time, however, the odor can mask your own scent from humans, allowing you to casually hang out until something tasty walks by.

7. **Behind Trees**. Find a good-sized tree that's larger than your width. From our past experiences, a tree that is smaller may not work as well.

8. **Sewers.** Storm drains, ditches, and gutters are usually within proximity of high-traffic areas such as parking lots and sidewalks. Lie down in the right one and you could snag yourself a street-side meal. However, as with trash cans, the sewer odor can decrease your zombie senses.

9. **Outbuildings.** Sheds, outhouses, chicken coops, and doghouses are all wonderful places to lay low. A human is bound to investigate when the family dog starts barking in the backyard. When the curious breather cracks open the door, unleash a world of hurt.

10. **Cemeteries.** How stereotypical, right? Wrong! Graveyards are filled with hundreds of headstones that are perfect to lurk behind. Eventually, someone's going to take a shortcut to death, and you'll be waiting to help them.

Human Structures

At some point during a successful zombie uprising, officials in the human government will broadcast warnings and possibly even issue a quarantine for the infected area, trapping plenty of the living in the hot zone. At this point, many humans will barricade themselves in houses, commercial buildings, or other man-made structures they perceive to be safe. Each type of structure, from an isolated farmhouse to a neighborhood pub, will require zombie entry strategies to bypass breathers' feeble attempts to stop us.

Houses

The word "house" is a generic term that describes human residences of all shapes and sizes. However different they may appear, most houses share structural similarities, such as doors, windows, roofs, and toilets. These dwellings, from the cardboard box to the Hampton mansion, are designed to satisfy the personal and emotional needs of the living.

Though humans build their homes with certain safeguards to keep out possible intruders, during an outbreak they often add additional fortifications to deter the infected. With only basic weekend warrior skills, breathers will board up windows, block entrances, and erect additional fencing. Some humans will sit in them quietly, hoping not to be noticed, while others will brazenly use weaponry for added defense. Most of these added measures can easily be bypassed by experienced undead soldiers—and, as mentioned earlier, they are a sure sign of recent human occupancy.

WE KILL
ZOMBIES

Review these illustrations of two single-family detached houses. With a quick glance, you will notice that *House 1* has been fortified with additional structures that could make entering it difficult. They are evidence that someone has prepared the house for the current epidemic. Very likely, the house will contain not only that someone and his or her loved ones but also other uninfected humans who were attracted there by the promise of safe refuge.

House 2 is noticeably different. A house that shows signs of forced entry, with open doors, broken windows, and other structural damage, is less likely to yield a warm meal. Because this pad's entry points are available and unobstructed, it provides *no* protection for the living.

So only House 1 is worth your attention. But how do you gain access to such a well-fortified home?

1. Ho ho ho, it's Zombie Santa! With dislocated joints and a slightly smaller decomposing body, it might be possible for you to shimmy down the chimney. If you smell smoke, abort the mission—a fire is waiting at the bottom, ready to ignite your rotten ass. Remember, cremation can be fatal.

2. Given your impaired dexterity, climbing to a second story window might be difficult, and humans will often assume that it's downright impossible. Most likely, they will leave this window relatively unfortified, making it an easy access point for zombie climbers.

3. Huffing and puffing will not blow the house down, but a zombie battering ram might! Grab the nearest zed or zed-terminated corpse and use it to break down the door.

4. During a zombie pandemic, homeowners are seldom able to locate a reliable contractor. A home's windows may appear to be boarded up, but it's very likely that someone tried to save some time and got stingy on the nails. Just yank the wood a bit to see if anything budges.

5. The old basement window trick. Humans will often run upstairs but neglect their basement defenses. Check the lowest windows, break the glass, then crawl or fall in.

6. Depending on the year and model, it might be possible to just lift a garage door open. If you don't find a vehicle, don't be fooled; an empty garage doesn't mean the house is empty.

7. The garage window is another area of the house that could have been neglected. Push, pull, and slide it, but if it doesn't budge, just start pounding. The noise of breaking glass may frighten the living out of hiding.

8. Use your head to smash the window in the garage's service door. A few head butts and you should fall right inside.

9. Depending on the house design, an additional entrance for the basement may be available around back—the perfect opening for a sneak attack.

10. Use what's available to gain entry. Patio furniture, bricks, stones, flowerpots, severed limbs, or other yard objects can easily break a window.

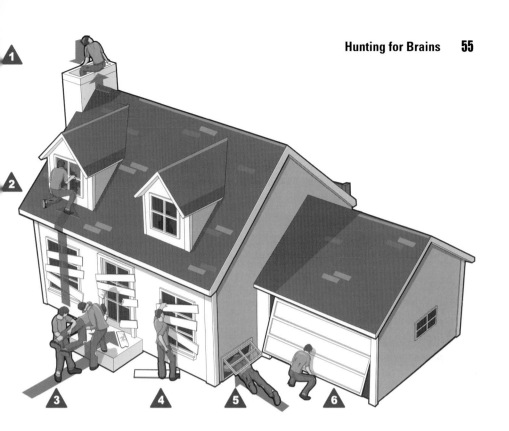

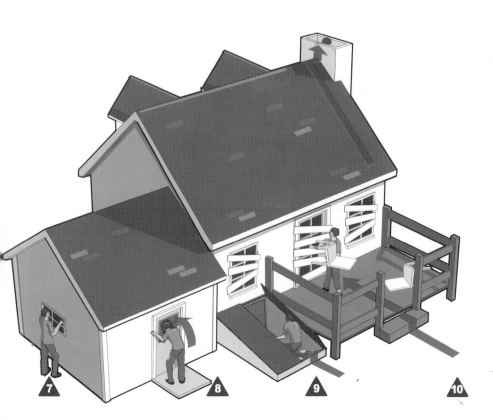

Commercial Buildings

What happens if Mr. and Ms. Brains are not home? We recommend the urban buffet located on Main Street. The commercial structures found there may range from simple storefronts to towering skyscrapers to dingy factories, and all of them are brain magnets during a z-virus infestation. Storefronts may hold the promise of much-needed food and supplies, skyscrapers offer the protection of dozens of flights of stairs and up-to-code security systems, and large factories feature additional fencing and steel-plated doors.

You never know what is lurking behind those closed doors during a siege. Is it a brewery or a weapons factory? But the unknown shouldn't be a repellent. Commercial structures often contain immense square footage and numerous entrances that are difficult to defend,

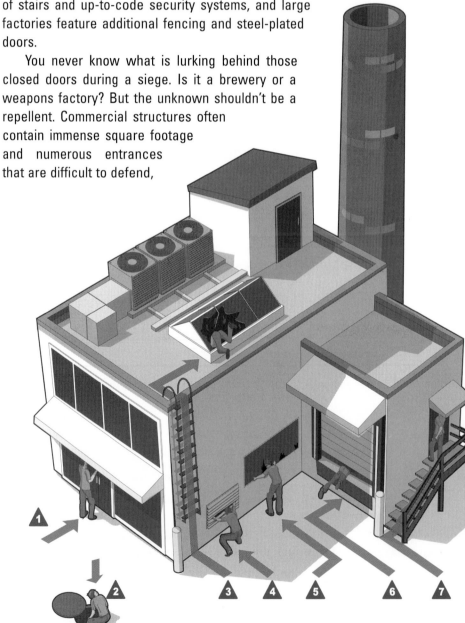

making these locations just as vulnerable as a house—with a possible higher brain return.

Commercial buildings present their own unique opportunities for zombie infiltration.

1. Tap on the glass—breathers love that! Smash the lobby window using your body or another object. Or, depending on your pre-zombie life, the lanyard noosing your neck could have a keycard for this exact building!

2. Industrial sewer systems are more than wide enough to accommodate your spoiled body. Remove manhole covers or storm drains in the vicinity of the property and you may discover a subterranean entrance into the building. But beware: if you're not careful you could become lost, only to reemerge from the sewers months later with an odor even fouler than when you went down.

3. For one out of every eight zombies, climbing a fire escape is possible (see "Ladder," page 60). If you are so equipped, once you reach the roof, try to access a rooftop door, or just plunge through a skylight.

4. Air vents: the unsecured entrance. Locate a sizeable vent and tear it open. Enter, and eventually you'll see the light at the end of the tin tunnel. You may find an even quicker entrance if the duct supports give way under your weight.

5. Windows in commercial buildings vary in many ways, including glass thickness. Most glass is eventually breakable; the windows of financial institutions are the exception.

6. Overrun the loading docks by crawling under the dock seals to gain access to the facility's warehouse bay. The humans will not expect you to bypass these doors, so the degree of resistance should be scant.

7. If accidentally left ajar, fire exits = zombie entrances. If securely shut, however, they will be impossible to pry open. Fire regulations often require them to be constructed of materials such as wire mesh glass that give them the strength of security armor.

Other Human Infrastructures

Now's the time to focus beyond your immediate brain lust. In time, humans will attempt to combat the zed invasion by developing weapons with innovative antizombie capabilities. But to create these devices, they will need access to electrical power and possibly global communication devices like radios and cell phones. You and your horde will have a greater chance of survival if you disrupt that access.

For example, consider the benefit of attacking the local nuclear power plant. Once the staff is eaten, either a safety system will automatically shut down the plant or a meltdown will occur, resulting in widespread nuclear devastation. Either way, you will suspend the plant's power output and disrupt human life far and wide, and perhaps attract more humans to the infected area to inspect the damage.

Other electronic utility structures are less fragile but no less vulnerable. Look for power lines, broadcast antennas, and cell phone towers, and disrupt their functionality by gnawing on any exposed wires. We know what you're thinking: won't this fry me? The quick answer is no. When the living are electrocuted, they experience all types of problems: nerve damage, slurred speech, memory loss, breathing irregularities, heart failure—all symptoms you already have! As long as your body hasn't dried out enough to instantly catch fire, a strong electrical current should be harmless.

So if you come across any of these utility silhouettes shown below, feel free to wreak zombie havoc.

Obstacles You Will Face

While on the hunt, you will encounter a mess of odd gadgets specifically designed to hinder any zed. Many of the contraptions will lure you in with their lustrous shine, then enrage you with a high degree of puzzlement. Mastering these obstacles may mean the difference between warm mouthfuls of human BLT (brain, liver, tendon) and rodent leftovers from the city park. Review the following do-it-yourself diagrams.

Doorknob

Doorknobs vary in style and location, and are responsible for securing doors shut. When encountering a closed door, your first response will be to bang on it. Wooden doors can crack or splinter. Glass doors are known to shatter. But if physical abuse proves useless, try rotating the knob as indicated. (Result may vary.)

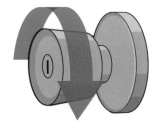 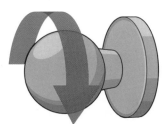 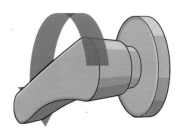

Ladder

Not all zombies are created equally; only one in eight zeds is capable of scaling a ladder or similar structure. And the number of rungs can be an issue—coordination varies from zed to zed. But if you or someone in your horde can climb a ladder, by all means do! Fire escapes or maintenance ladders fixed to buildings are common, so look for these pathways to the brains.

Stairs

By employing their arms and/or legs, most zeds are capable of climbing staircases. If this weren't possible, newly reanimated zombies could never stand up in the first place. As you climb stairs, you may experience balance issues, resulting in nonfatal falls. Simply dust yourself off and continue the pursuit.

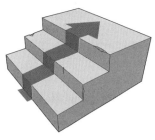

Your average zombie-busting human will have a difficult time destroying a wooden staircase, but he or she can certainly block one. Do your best to remove obstacles by tearing into rubble or swan diving over it.

Fence

Fences are a real kick in the rotten balls! Most are designed to restrict access. Scaling them can be tantalizing but is often beyond the average zed's dexterity—it's often easier to plow right through. You'll find your greatest success with fences that are approximately your height or lower, and fences constructed out of wood. The chain-link variety, often used as a mobile barricade and topped with barbed wire, will be virtually impossible for you to pass over; just go around.

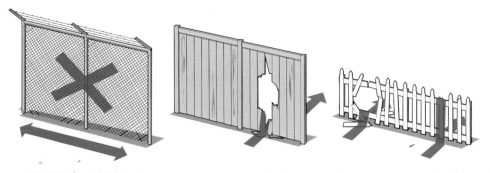

Tree

If a human climbs a tree to escape you, can you climb up after him? Unfortunately, you probably can't. The good news is, you don't even need to! If you're patient, eventually you will starve the breather out of the limbs. Seriously, how many provisions can a human store in a tree? Or, with sufficient moaning, enough zeds may swarm the tree to cause a zombie pileup, forming a ramp that will get the top zombie in range of your victim.

Rope

Rope climbing is impossible for zombies, so unless you want to relive some high school gym class fantasy, don't even try. But, again, what's the rush? What goes up will have to come down. So unless another meal catches your rotten eye, just wait it out—your victim can't hang on forever.

Terrain Types

While hunting, you will sometimes follow a human into an unfamiliar location. This may be an area of extreme cold, extreme warmth, or extreme moisture, any of which can have a serious impact on your bodily integrity. Before boldly going where no zed has gone before, review the dangers outlined below.

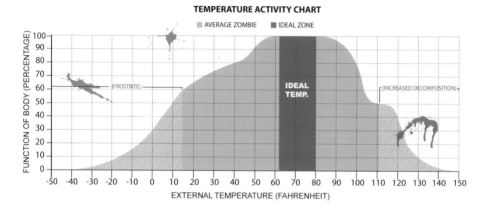

TEMPERATURE ACTIVITY CHART

AVERAGE ZOMBIE   IDEAL ZONE

X-axis: EXTERNAL TEMPERATURE (FAHRENHEIT) — -50 -40 -30 -20 -10 0 10 20 30 40 50 60 70 80 90 100 110 120 130 140 150

Y-axis: FUNCTION OF BODY (PERCENTAGE) — 0 10 20 30 40 50 60 70 80 90 100

(FROSTBITE)   IDEAL TEMP.   (INCREASED DECOMPOSITION)

Cold

Remember the Beringia land bridge (see page 6)? Trying to walk in snow is the least of your worries.

The z-virus is very good at regulating your body's temperature, keeping it steady at around 70° F, but this ability to thermoregulate decreases as temperatures fall. At very low temperatures, the z-virus in you will increase your cellular absorption and decomposition to keep your internal temperature at acceptable levels. Over a long period of time, your muscles will become less responsive and less elastic, leading to coordination problems and slowing down your bodily functions. Your speed may slow by as much as half, and with food more difficult to find and chase, you may decompose to immobility.

If you experience an extreme freeze, 15° F or below, your body will be vulnerable to frostbite (a type of decay), but your extremities should continue to function until they fall off. Don't be alarmed unless your eyelids freeze shut. If you are that cold, eventually your body will completely stiffen up. A zombie body that has been frozen for longer than 48 hours will be use-

less when thawed. Water in its cells will expand during freezing and destroy the body's infrastructure, rendering it limp when warmed up.

Warmth

Extreme heat (110° F or above) can also affect your body. In some parts of the globe, temperatures can reach an astounding 150° F. How does this affect you? As molecules heat up in a humid environment, they increase their movement, leading to cell breakdown. Depending on the humidity, your rate of decomposition can double as the temperature rises. As a result, your body will need to double its nutritional intake of human flesh (see "Human Buffet," page 105). But if the temperature is high and the humidity low, decomposition will be halted. That is a *good* thing.

Water

The lifeguard has been eaten!

As you've read, moisture and humidity will increase tissue breakdown. So what does swimming do? Zeds that spend too much time in water will experience rapid decomposition. Early signs of this included pruning up of the toxic skin. Stay dry! Avoid prolonged exposure to water, including rain. Also, don't continually roam sewers or other subterranean domains, as these damp environments will also accelerate decomposition.

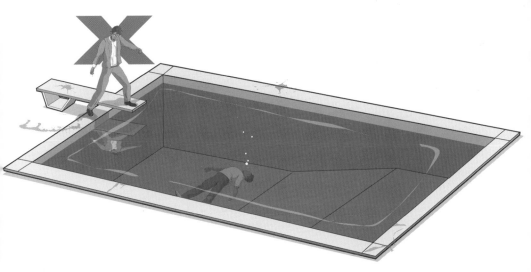

I See a Human—What Should I Do?

Now that you've learned the basics of hunting, you're bound to come across your first human. Awesome—this is what being a zombie is all about!

So let out a moan to announce to the horde that dinner has been located. Within seconds, the mob will shift gears and zero in on your find.

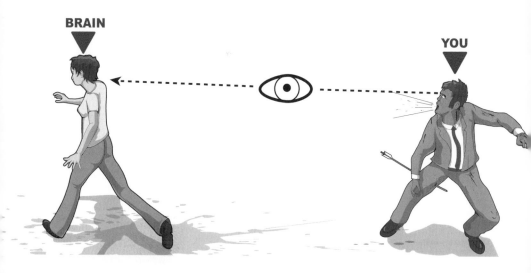

5

TRANSPORTATION

In the past, stubborn Luddite zombies ignored the technological changes in the world of the living. They even underestimated the significance of the automobile, an advancement in transportation technology with which zeds must frequently contend. With roughly 700 million of these monsters on the road, humans are positively obsessed with them. And their obsession only increases during an outbreak, since these vehicles are perfect for both shielding the living from our attacks and carrying them out of the contaminated zone. So unless you are hunting the Amish, hunting strategies that were used against the chariot and the stagecoach are obsolete. It's time to learn how to take down the auto.

The living would have us believe their automobiles are impenetrable. However, this is a total deception—they are full of vulnerabilities!

- Many cars, foreign and domestic, can easily be stopped with minimal collateral damage. (See "How to Stop a Vehicle," below.)
- From what we know, they all rely on fuel, which limits their range.
- They are mechanically complicated—just look at them—and often break down unexpectedly. Better still, the average human does not know how to repair them.
- Most require a key to operate, and when humans panic, they are highly likely to flee to a car without bringing the key with them.
- They are very noisy. Zombies can hear their engines and mufflers from miles away.

How to Stop a Vehicle

How many zombies does it take to stop a car? In truth, only one! Humans won't stop their cars for a minor obstruction in the roadway—just ask any squirrel—and they certainly won't stop for a crossing zombie. But if you stumble in front of a vehicle at the right moment, you can easily cause a wreck.

At what price, though? Your body could sustain cranial damage in the process, impairing your ability to feed. The whole point of stopping a car is to feast on the humans inside, so keep your eye on the prize and avoid being the appointed crash test dummy. Here are several better methods for stopping a vehicle.

The Jump

In this strategy, you penetrate the driver's side windshield and obstruct the operator's view of the road. Statistically speaking, it's best accomplished around dusk for lowest human visibility. Choose a narrow street (rural or urban) to increase accuracy and the element of surprise. Patiently wait off to the side, or behind a number of obstacles abandoned on the road. Then, when you hear an approaching vehicle, stumble out directly in its path. Though most zombies are incapable of actually jumping, the impact will propel your body like a speeding missile, embedding your head and torso into the windshield. This will cause the driver to panic, causing a wreck or, at the very least, emergency braking.

This method is still extremely hazardous: three out of five zombies experience cranial trauma during the Jump. Reread the last sentence so you know what you're getting into.

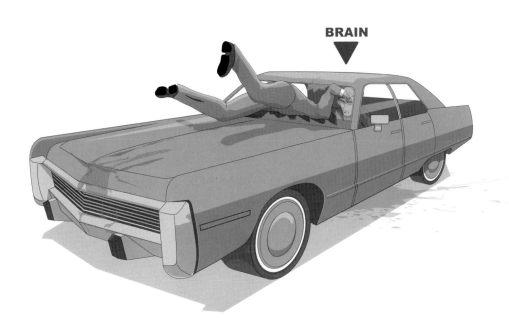

Body Bag Roadblock

During a serious zombie outbreak, human defenders will need ammunition, food, and other supplies on the front lines, so supply lines will be critical. Set up a temporary roadblock by using a large mob of the undead. This barricade will be both intimidating and fatal to anyone who dares to ram it.

With hundreds of infectious jaws and flailing appendages, your numbers will quickly overpower most automobiles, giving you access to the supply of brains inside. But the Body Bag Roadblock does come with a price: collateral damage is unavoidable. Position yourself toward the rear of the unruly mob.

Undead Traffic Stop

What is it about someone in uniform that captures everyone's attention? If you're lucky, your horde will include a few zombified emergency personnel, still sporting their official ensembles. We have found that human drivers will stop for assistance if they spot a uniformed official on a road standing by the appropriate vehicle—an abandoned one shouldn't be too hard to find.

Of course, motorists will eventually realize that the officer is a zombie and quickly speed away. However, if the driver stops the vehicle first, or even just reduces speed, it provides an opportunity for an assault by the uniformed zed or a zed party waiting in the shadows.

Wounded Roadkill

Do Good Samaritans exist during a zombie outbreak? Probably not, but we will continue to test that theory.

For this tactic to work, a well-dressed, fresh zed should position its body facedown on the side of the road. All rotten flesh should be concealed, as faded green skin is an obvious sign that you are undead. Eventually, a vehicle racing out of infected territory will approach. The "victim" should move slightly to indicate that he or she is still "alive." If the driver does step out to investigate, attack! However, it is very possible that a fleeing survivor will see through the ruse and take the opportunity to run you over, so don't lie in the middle of the road.

Car Chase

What have we told you about chasing cars? Nothing yet—but chasing cars can actually help you secure your prey! You and your horde can distract the driver enough to cause a wreck worthy of Hollywood. Road obstacles and curvy roads increase the chances of causing a successful accident.

Depending on the speed of the vehicle, your reanimated muscles might eventually tear to the point of affecting your mobility, so don't overexert yourself. In addition, watch out for random shots being fired from the vehicles (see "Avoiding the Bullet," page 84).

Werezombies—undead werewolves—excel at car chasing. They have been known to exceed 55 MPH before incurring severe muscle damage.

Human Extraction

Hey, it actually worked—you stopped a vehicle! Now you need to extract your victims. Penetrating the outer defenses of a common civilian vehicle can be done quite easily. The following illustration and instructions provide a few quick tips on how to get access to a car's soft insides.

1. **Windshield Head Bang.** Depending on how you stopped the vehicle, you might already be stuck through the windshield. Chomp your jaws and watch the mass exodus. Then free yourself and go after them!

2. **Window Pull.** Smash out a side window if possible. Grab onto your victim and yank him or her out through the broken glass—the smell of blood will drive you crazy (see "Holding Techniques," page 80).

3. **Roof Punch.** Is the car a soft-top convertible? Soft tops are made out of vinyl or canvas and can easily be scratched or bitten through.

4. **Back Window.** Frequently smashed in the wreck or shot out with bullets, the back window provides the perfect access to the backseat. Once inside, go for their necks.

5. **Rip the Damn Doors Off.** One of the car's doors could be damaged from the wreck. Give it a jerk. You can usually terrify the living by ripping doors off anything.

How to Hitch a Ride

Need to go somewhere? Hunting for brains with limited success can take its toll. As breathers are disposed of, brain resources will be depleted and probably won't be replaced. It's time for a change of scenery. Hitching a ride on an unsuspecting vehicle might be your meal ticket to new hunting grounds.

During an outbreak, most vehicles will be racing toward refugee camps and other uncontaminated areas, all full of fresh meat. With a little luck, you might snag a one-way ticket to one of these promised lands, with fresh brains as far as the zed can see. Turn the page for a few zombie hitchhiking tips.

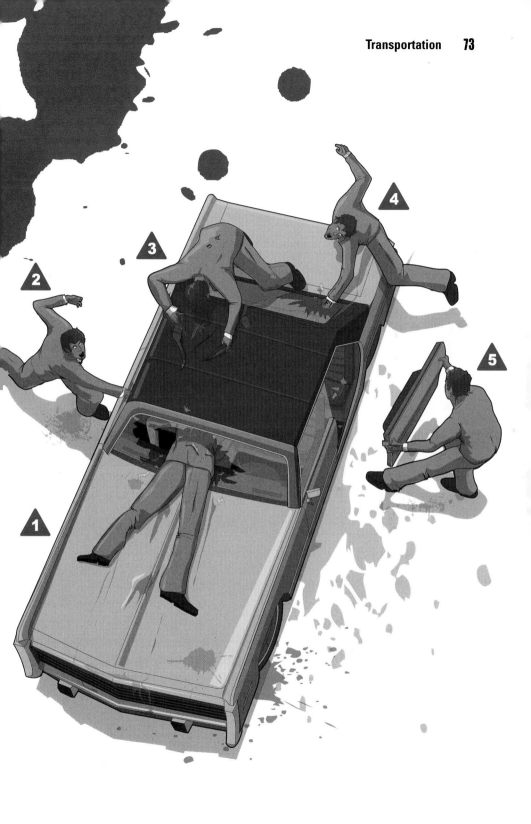

Roof Surfing

When it comes to roof surfing, the bigger the vehicle the better. Delivery vehicles, buses, and semi trucks all have ample room to hang out on top. You can gain access to your ride by crawling up the back or dropping on top from above, but keep quiet so as not to reveal your presence. Continue your journey until you see, smell, or hear a large population of brains. Roll off and go to work.

Frame Hold

As the driver stops to raid a convenience store or defecate along the roadside, crawl under the vehicle and find something to hang onto. As soon as the breather is done doing whatever breathers do, he or she will jump back in and drive away. Your body will be subjected to harsh abrasion caused by the road surface, but it's worth it. Eventually you'll gain access through a checkpoint. Once inside the safe zone, unleash hell.

Bumper Drag

Subtlety has never been the zombie's strong point, so why start now? While you're certain to be discovered by the next passing motorist, just hang onto the back bumper for as long as you can. You will experience all types of motions that may dislodge your grip, but every mile you make it is one less mile you have to walk. Word of caution: you may lose your shoes.

Cargo Bay

Trucks, trains, planes, and even ships have cargo bays. Because they are not designed to hold the living, these areas are usually only lightly supervised, perfect for settling right in for the long haul. Position your zed body around or in cargo that will help hide you from the occasional security check until you have arrived. What you do at your final destination is your own damn business, but we suggest terrorizing.

Rides to Avoid

Some vehicles are highly specialized and won't be used by the common human. Many of these vehicles are heavily built and could be armed with weaponry in support of the human resistance.

Some of our stopping techniques have been found to work on these vehicles, but most efforts will fail. When confronting a tank, armored car, or snow plow, zombie casualties will increase. The good news is, the breathers can't stay inside forever; eventually these vehicles will need to refuel or replenish supplies, and then we've got them.

Carefully review the eye chart on the next page. The vehicle pictured should be approached with extreme caution.

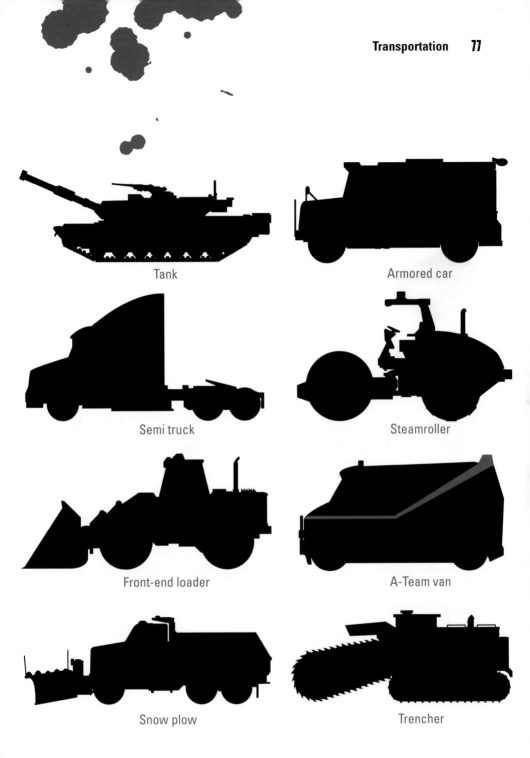

Tank

Armored car

Semi truck

Steamroller

Front-end loader

A-Team van

Snow plow

Trencher

One-Brain Vehicles

Single-brained vehicles are quick and small, making them difficult to catch. Many of them, including ATVs, dirt bikes, and big, red three-wheelers, are designed to handle all types of terrain. While they are superior in maneuverability, they are zed-vulnerable due to their open-cockpit design. Because the riders are exposed, they can easily be snared by a quick grab or projectile vomiting to the face. Sometimes you don't even need to touch them—use basic scare tactics to distract riders into losing their balance or control, causing them to crash.

Due to the sizes of these vehicles, hitchhiking is not possible.

ATV

Snowmobile

Dirt bike

Motorcycle

Moped

Bicycle

6

ATTACKING

Using the hunting strategies in the previous chapters, you'll be able to successfully track down your brainy target. What next? In order to subdue a living body for feasting, you need another plan of action.

Although only a small percentage of the living are prepared for living-on-undead combat, and most will ultimately fall before the zombie horde, that doesn't mean a battle can't be dangerous for you, the individual zombie. Humans possess an intense survival instinct, and when panic boosts their adrenaline, they're capable of desperate feats of strength that can catch even the hardiest zombie off guard. Being slightly more coordinated than you, humans may wield makeshift weaponry and employ nontraditional fighting strategies—expect them to shoot at you, burn you, and impale you with pointy sticks.

Nevertheless, when most zombies attack a human, they prefer to whale away blindly, disregarding any physical damage their target inflicts on them in return. From past zombie experiences, we've realized this probably isn't the best approach. Since our undead bodies don't heal from injury, self-preservation is very important.

Yes, the undead instinct is always "Bite first, ask questions later," but if you aren't careful, that strategy can lead to your demise. Mastering a few simple self-defense strategies, including "weapons of the body," will not only surprise the humans but also possibly impress your fellow zeds.

"ATTACK ANYTHING, FEAR NOTHING"

Holding Techniques

You've worked hard to find your prey, so you'd hate to lose it! The most basic attack strategy is holding a victim against his or her will. A properly executed hold will give you the opportunity to employ the other nasty strategies found in this chapter. Briefly study this illustration of the four most effective holds: the Hair Hold, the Bite Hold, the Arm Hold, and the Leg Hold.

Use Your Body as a Weapon

Your body is bursting with all types of bloodthirsty weaponry that can be used against the living. And remember: your flesh and blood are highly infectious. Once your victim is infected with the z-virus, he or she will begin to experience all types of nasty symptoms, weakening resistance and making it easier for you to gorge out. You can increase the likelihood of viral transference by biting, scratching, spitting, bleeding, and/or vomiting on your target.

The following diagram illustrates the deadliest weapons in your personal arsenal.

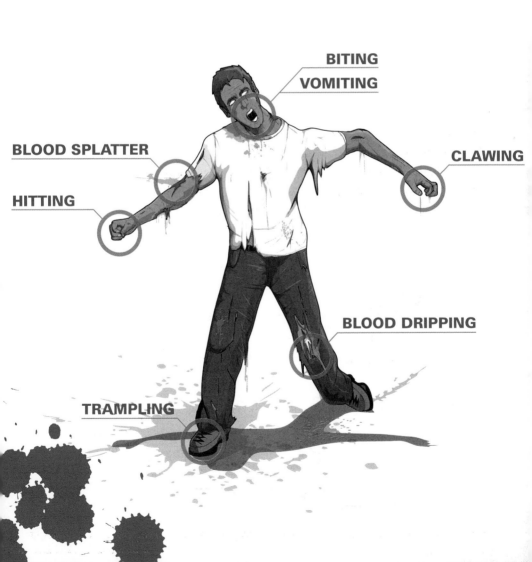

Biting

Your bite is mightier than your moan! Using your teeth, bite down on your victim's flesh, hard enough to tear through the skin. This will cause direct fluid-to-fluid contact. If you are a severely decomposed zombie, you may have experienced tooth loss. Your rotten gums may not break the skin's surface, making your mouth a less effective weapon.

Projectile Vomiting

Heaving toxic fluid from your stomach allows the possibility of attack at a distance. It can weaken your victim through infection, disorientation, or disgust, and can also cause temporary blindness. One out of four zombies is capable of projectile vomiting to a distance of six to seven feet.

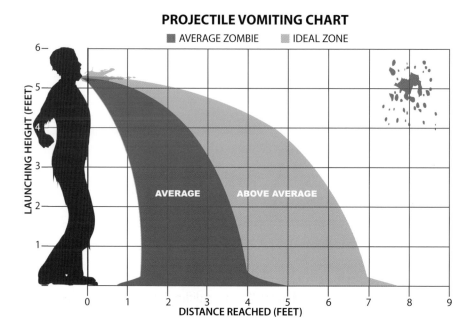

PROJECTILE VOMITING CHART

Clawing

At the ends of your fingers are fingernails, made up of a tough protein called keratin. These popular zombie weapons, randomly sharpened by breaks and chips, can easily pierce your victim's soft skin. When attacking for the kill, the more lacerations the more blood loss.

You should concentrate on clawing around your prey's neck. If you cut the jugular vein, it can lead to fatal hemorrhaging. Clawing the victim's head can also impair his or her vision, and possibly cause a concussion.

Enjoy your fingernails while you still can; eventually you will lose them due to severe decomposition.

Zed Melee Weapons

Along with their biological weapons (their bodies), certain zombies are capable of using primitive external weapons. If chimpanzees can, why can't zeds?

Most advanced weapons require study and training to use. In other words, they're too complicated for a zed. However, melee weapons, designed for close combat, can be effective without any technical know-how, just random arm motions.

Blunt Weapons

A blunt weapon is an edgeless, rounded, or unsharpened object used to inflict blunt force trauma. Clubs, pipes, logs, and severed body parts are all classified as blunt weapons. Tightly grab one of these items and haphazardly swing it around. Amputated appendages can be used to harm your victim psychologically as well as physically.

Edged Weapons

An edged weapon has two ends, the edge and the handle. If you carelessly handle the wrong end, you could lose a finger. Grab onto the non-shiny part before operating. These weapons usually require some training, but your abnormal shuffling and twitching will make it difficult for your victim to avoid being lacerated.

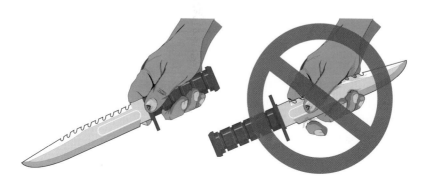

Projectile Weapons

You can quickly turn an ordinary object into a dangerous projectile by tossing it through the air, a technique best used during a siege. Glass fortifications can sometimes be demolished by chucking living and nonliving objects into them.

But now the bad news: 7 out of 10 zombies are incapable of throwing an object, and of the 3 who can, only 1 can hit its intended target.

Defensive Strategies

Past attempts at initiating a zombie apocalypse have always failed miserably. We know now that one of our biggest blunders has been our lack of defensive strategies. A zombie never retreats, only attacks—but better to attack in a way that limits the possibility of cranial injury and re-death. By studying thousands of failed engagements between humans and long-gone zeds, we have identified some of the most common attacks scenarios implemented by the living, and learned how to most effectively counter them.

Most humans are predictable—they usually go for your head. They have crafted all types of weapons to do this, but most often they rely on firearms. In certain situations, they may resort to fire or melee weapons instead, and either of these weapons can also cause cranial damage.

Review the following defensive strategies for the most common human attacks, and with a little luck you will avoid the embarrassing fate of our zombie forebears. Need more motivation? It's quite possible these trigger-happy humans used to be your buddies! Such behavior from an ex is understandable, but family and friends—what gives?

Avoiding the Bullet

Head shots are a bitch! A bullet targeted to the brain will cause almost certain death. Slow as you are, it is highly unlikely you can avoid a bullet traveling as fast as four thousand feet per second. Your best protection is avoiding gunfire altogether.

Of course, that isn't always possible. If they can, the living will certainly stockpile sufficient firepower to protect themselves and possibly hunt you down. Fortunately, as mentioned earlier (see "Terrible with Weapons," page 35), most humans are not trained marksmen and will unload rounds wildly, desperately trying to land a lucky shot between your eyes. These cowboy antics are as likely to hit other humans as they are you. Unfortunately, other breathers are trained snipers, waiting for a trophy zombie to kill. Until you have a chance to observe the shooter's technique, it will be very difficult to know the skill level of the target you are about to engage.

When being fired upon, you must avoid shots in both the Kill Box and the Deadly Triangle areas. A shot to the Kill Box is 99.9 percent fatal. Trained marksmen also aim at the Deadly Triangle, which if hit will result in an undead fatality. Head areas outside these kill zones are capable of absorbing minor blows without lasting effect, though if strong enough the hits could cause unconsciousness for 1 to 10 minutes. Severe damage to the upper spinal cord, the brain stem area, could also result in termination.

In short, guns are bad news. If you see a human holding one of the firearms depicted here, implement one of the following bullet-avoidance attack strategies. Remember, even after being bitten, your victim still is capable of firing a weapon, so once you've employed a maneuver it is important to disarm (or remove the arm of) the shooter to avoid a scuffle shot.

KILL BOX

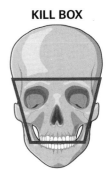

DEADLY TRIANGLE

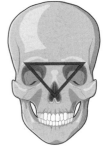

Diamond Attack

The Diamond Attack, also called the Zombie Wedge, is used to move directly and quickly toward an armed human. If a Diamond Attack maneuver succeeds, the human target will only have time to take down the lead zombies posing the most imminent danger before the distance between the two forces closes and the remaining zombie in the rear can quickly overtake its target.

For obvious reasons, the ideal role in this maneuver is to be the zombie in the back. Once you reach your victim, engage in biting combat. Results may vary with the number of human targets, ammunition supply, and firing accuracy.

Flanking Zeds

A swarm attack, better known as Flanking Zeds, is a tactical maneuver used by a horde during a frontal attack. In it, zeds attack their target from several directions. Swarming from different positions, they force their enemy to defend two or three sides at once, overwhelming him or her.

Employing Flanking Zeds also reduces the maneuverability of the living and reduces the chance that a similar flanking tactic could be used against the horde. With both a physical and psychological advantage, victory is possible.

The Zombie Shield

With the Zombie Shield, you protect your own body by using another corpse to absorb bullets fired at you. Snatch up a lifeless "volunteer" and position him or her directly between you and the living human's weapon. Hold tightly to your protective armor until you've closed the distance between you and the shooter. Once you're within striking distance, throw the body at your prey while you lunge mouth-first at him or her.

Zedcoy

The Zedcoy maneuver is designed to distract the living while a hidden zombie party executes a surprise attack. The decoy zombie captures the attention of your target by screaming, vomiting, charging, or throwing something. While the zedcoy begins absorbing shots, a second group attacks from behind.

This strategy may sound simple, but with all our random moaning and clumsiness, it's unlikely that the second group will be able to approach the victim in complete silence. The louder and more threatening the zedcoy, the better. A fast zedcoy also increases the chances of success, as it reduces the shooter's opportunity for successful head shots.

Encircle

Attacking from every direction simultaneously will overwhelm your victim with potential targets while reducing his or her maneuverability. Tactically, it sounds ideal, but with the human firing at random zeds, it could quickly turn into an unfriendly game of Russian Roulette. Ensure that the shooter is a poor shot before proceeding.

This tactic has also been given the name Snack Attack, because with so many zombies, each attacker's portion of human flesh will be small (see "The Zombie Code," page 143). Everyone will have their dirty little fingers in your dirty little human pie.

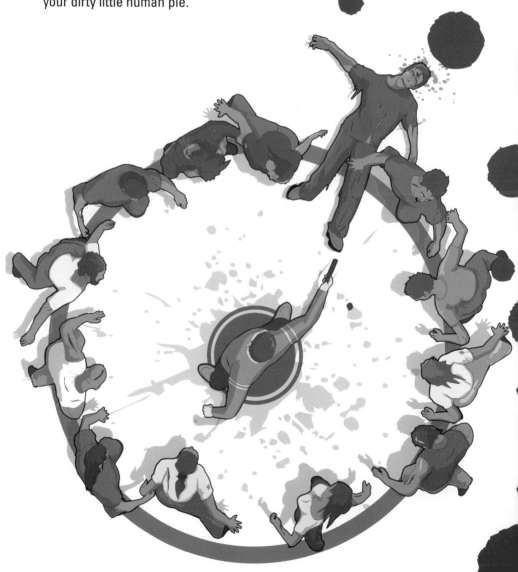

Aerial Fall

Zombies away! An Aerial Fall will be completely unexpected by any mortal playing cowboy in the streets beneath a high-rise. In order to gain the tactical advantage of height, you will first have to master the obstacle of stairs (see "Obstacles You Will Face," page 59). Climb up a story or two (any higher and you risk a fatal fall), and wait until your victim is directly below you. Then quietly plummet to the ground and squash your prey.

The impact should severely injure your target, or at least disorient him. After that, inject your teeth into your landing cushion.

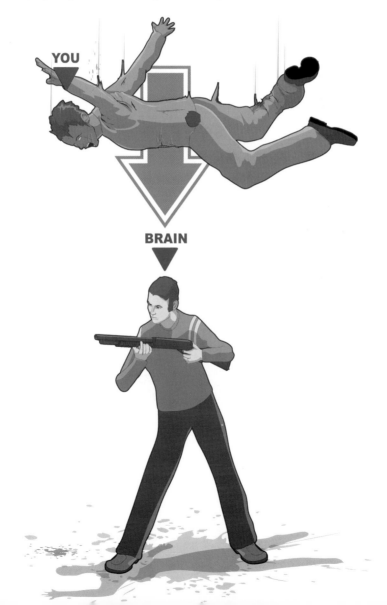

The Flame

When humans play with fire, be prepared to be burned!

Fire has always captured the attention of zeds on the prowl. We are mentally incapable of starting a fire of any kind (on purpose), so fire is usually associated with the presence of the living, who use it for cooking, heating, and illumination. Once humans get a fire burning, flickering flames or plumes of smoke can easily be spotted at great distances. Even if our vision is hampered by blocked sightlines or facial damage, our zombie noses can still smell the smoke. Once alerted, we can rarely resist advancing in the direction of the fire.

Our infatuation can be problematic, though, as humans have been known to use fire as a weapon. True, flames can't cause us pain, but does this mean that they have no effect on us? Sorry to say, but recorded attacks have proven they do; your brain can very easily be cooked. A dried-up, severely decomposed zed can be incinerated in just a few minutes, while a fresh zombie can last nearly half an hour before being reduced to ashes. But even if you outlast the flames, body parts that have been damaged stay damaged. What's more, smoke is rarely a successful medium for spreading the z-virus.

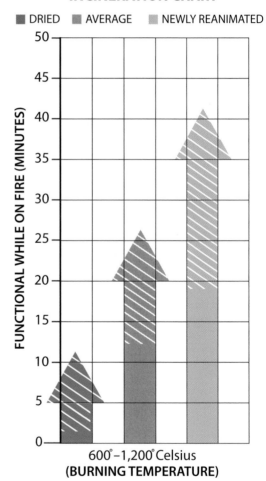

INCINERATION CHART

■ DRIED   ■ AVERAGE   ▨ NEWLY REANIMATED

FUNCTIONAL WHILE ON FIRE (MINUTES)

600°–1,200° Celsius
(BURNING TEMPERATURE)

Most humans will conserve flammable fuels during an outbreak, but they might spare some to incinerate a zombie when necessary. Commit the arson tools shown below to memory. If you observe one of them in the hands of a human, put into action one of the following fire strategies. Some of these strategies can also be used against corrosive acids.

Drench March

Most zombies are completely incapable of recognizing the smell of gasoline or other volatile fuels (diesel oil, kerosene, etc.), and the resistance knows it, those pyrohuman bastards! They have adopted two successful tactics to exploit this weakness. The first and more common is to pour a pool of flammable liquid on the ground, lure us into it, and set it ablaze from a distance. The second, generally used as a last-ditch option, is simply to throw the liquid at us and ignite us. If either of these things happens, you should keep moving toward your target. That's why this tactic is known as the Drench March.

Yes, your clothing will quickly catch fire and melt to your skin. But keep in mind that the only thing more lethal than you is you on fire! If you're blazing, don't hesitate—attack! You could very well spread the fire, hampering the defenses of the living. One of the best-recorded zombie fire attacks caused the Great Chicago Fire of 1871. Eventually the inferno destroyed four square miles of breather territory. Humans blamed the blaze on Mrs. O'Leary's cow—how utterly ridiculous.

Fire Composure

Some fire will knock you on your ass! Military flamethrowers are capable of propelling a burst of flammable liquid over one hundred feet. These back-pack models are currently out of service, though many are in the hands of private collectors.

If you do encounter a flamethrower, the flames will likely burn your eyes, detrimentally affecting your vision. And even if the flamethrower misses you, the burst of illumination can still cause temporary blindness. It's important to maintain your "fire composure." Once ignited, keep your balance and continue in the direction you last saw your target.

Molotov Bypass

During a battle, you'll experience all types of homemade fire grenades. The most common is the Molotov cocktail. Made out of a glass bottle filled with flammable fuels and a cloth wick, it explodes into flames on impact.

The Molotov Bypass is the study of a burning missile's trajectory. While the device is in the air, you estimate its point of impact and shuffle away from the surrounding area.

In truth, this is not a good strategy. You really shouldn't alter your course of attack. Any human who is capable of hitting you with a bottle is already in eatable distance. Flaming or not, shamble on. Make your junior anarchist reconsider his or her profession.

Hand-to-Mouth Combat

Advanced though they are, firearms and flame weapons still have their problems. Supplies of ammunition and fuel will run out during an extended zombie uprising, forcing the living to resort to the melee weapons of the past.

Ancient breathers developed the spear around 400,000 years ago. It was very popular and effective against animal targets, but it proved useless against the ancient zombie. So humans developed more sophisticated weapons designed to decapitate the undead, such as the ax and the sword. Eventually, however, they realized that attacking at a distance was the best way to avoid accidental infection. So around 1300 A.D., the brains-at-arms developed the firearm. This new weapon made the battle-ax and sword obsolete. The ax evolved into a tool. The sword's fate was much grimmer; today it is sold as decorative art on TV shopping networks.

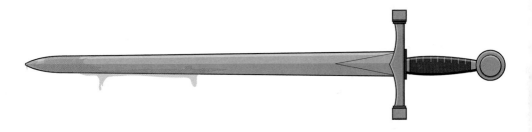

If a desperate human pulls one of these melee weapons out of retirement, you have little to worry about. Most of them are relatively harmless to you, with a low chance of inflicting cranial injury. They are all designed for close combat, which means you'll be within arm's reach of your meal before you're in any danger. Once in close proximity, resort to biting, scratching, and spitting to slow and subdue your target. In the end, all such confrontations will eventually lead to hand-to-mouth combat.

Review the melee weapons in the chart on the next page. If your target is holding onto one of these objects, use the following attack strategies to prevail in the final struggle.

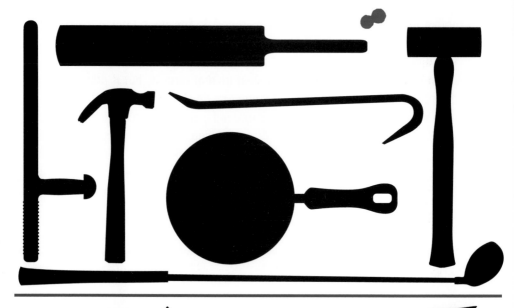

Erratic Attack

In the Erratic Attack, also known as the Zombie Gait, you move with inconsistent motion toward your attacker, keeping your head slightly tilted. With a lowered head and unpredictable motion, you will decrease your adversary's targeting accuracy. Flailing your arms can also improve this defensive strategy.

If the target still manages to land a blow to your head but it's not strong enough to crush your skull or decapitate you, proceed. Always proceed!

Chopping Block

It is not impossible to defend against a sword. When you approach within a corpse's length of your prey, fall headfirst into your target's knees or thighs. This will greatly disrupt his or her sword-swinging form, making a clean decapitation difficult. Before the human can readjust or execute a second swing, clench and maul his or her leg.

If you forget to execute the Chopping Block maneuver, all is not lost. Most swords are incapable of cutting bones. Even if your flesh is cut, you can survive partial decapitation if the brain stem remains intact.

Forearm Shield

If you position your arms in front of your face, you will shield your unprotected neck from sharp-edged weapons. The Forearm Shield can result in lost appendages, but it's a small price to pay to avoid decapitation. Take the hit and proceed.

Expect additional damage to your center of mass or lower extremities, both of which might slow you down. Edged weapons that impale your flesh are likely to stay lodged in your body for extended periods of time. Significant protruding handles and arrows can snag on objects and increase body damage. Shamble with care.

Ghoul Reach

Borrowed from our supernatural siblings the mummies, the Ghoul Reach has been used successfully for thousands of years. By extending your arms in front of your body, you decrease your opponent's access to your neck or head.

Once your arms are extended, use your hands to claw, scratch, or latch onto your victim. For unknown reasons, the Ghoul Reach tends to increase moaning.

Combat Quiz

1. Someone just stabbed a knife in my back. I should . . .

    a) Seek medical attention immediately!

    b) Get over it, and continue with what I am doing.

    c) Fall down to ease the pain.

    d) Have a fellow Zed remove it.

2. Someone just set me on fire. What should I do?

    a) Retreat back into the zombie mob.

    b) Search for water.

    c) Continue attacking.

    d) Extinguish it with flammable fuel.

3. I'm being shot at, but they can't hit squat. I should . . .

    a) Use the Zombie Shield technique.

    b) Implement the Ghoul Reach.

    c) Retreat.

    d) Defecate in my pants.

4. He's holding a *katana* sword!

    a) Do not engage and look for an exit strategy!

    b) Play dead.

    c) Execute the Chopping Block on that mofo.

    d) Look for your own sword or appendage to duel.

5. Melee weapon include . . .

a) Pickaxes.

b) Metal pipes.

c) Machetes.

d) All the above.

6. I've encountered many humans with multiple weapons. I should . . .

a) Seek reinforcements.

b) Surrender by waving a white cloth.

c) Not be intimidated, and attack.

d) Run and hide.

7

HUMAN BUFFET

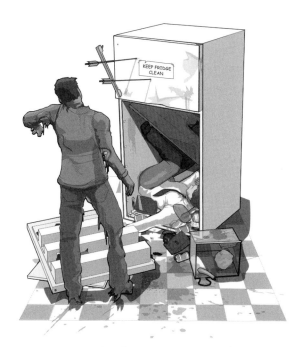

You've hunted and subdued a human target, and now comes the main event—it's feeding time!

As mentioned earlier, your hunger for living flesh is more than an unquenchable craving. It's a biological necessity. Contrary to popular human belief, the undead body still relies on the food in its digestive tract to function. But instead of using specialized organs to extract energy and nutrients, the tract now acts as a holding cavity. As flesh passes through the tract, the z-virus absorbs the acids of some of the 10 trillion cells found in the living body. This creates the energy the virus needs to stave off decomposition (see "Post-life Expectancy," page 28).

Because a zed that stops feeding will slowly starve to complete decomposition, and because living food is often difficult to obtain, the z-virus must encourage its host to hunt relentlessly to ensure its own survival. During the reanimation process, your brain underwent mutation. The virus modified the region of the brain that regulates feeding so that it constantly stimulates the body's hunger signals. The result is that you're always hungry for . . . well, you know the rest.

The Preferable Flesh

Zeds are capable of consuming a wide variety of live flesh, no matter what the size, species, or hairball risk. But although you can make do eating other animals during down time, for maximum nutritional value we encourage you to feed on the number one zombie delicacy: fresh human brain tissue, pinkish on the outside and white on the inside.

So, what's so special about the human brain? It's filled with billions of highly specialized sensory cells brimming with electrochemical pulses. When consumed, these particular cells create an intense concentration of biological energy, significantly reducing your monthly flesh requirements. A few bites of brain and you'll suddenly feel what is called a *medulla rush*, an adrenaline burst that increases your mobility.

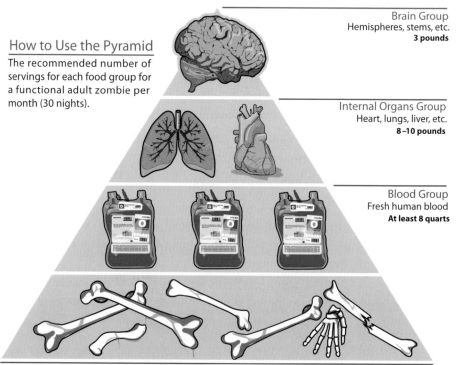

Brain Group
Hemispheres, stems, etc.
3 pounds

How to Use the Pyramid
The recommended number of servings for each food group for a functional adult zombie per month (30 nights).

Internal Organs Group
Heart, lungs, liver, etc.
8–10 pounds

Blood Group
Fresh human blood
At least 8 quarts

Bone Marrow Group   Tissue found in the hollow interior of bones - **30–40 Servings**

This zombie food pyramid suggests the number of servings of brain and other human meat you should consume per month for optimal nutrition. The chart is based on the average-sized human; if dining on children, adjust quantities accordingly.

Your life expectancy will greatly increase as your energy intake from human flesh increases. However, gorging can lead to a ruptured stomach, so it is important that you eat responsibly. In addition, rotten meat and aged blood can prove fatal. Bodies that have been dead longer than 12 hours should generally not be consumed. Higher and lower temperatures may decrease or increase this timeframe; use your zombie senses to make a final determination of freshness (see "Rotten Is a No-No," page 112).

Brain Group

You haven't really "died" until you've tried human brain! Even though it only accounts for 2 percent of your victim's body weight, it represents the most important group on the Zombie Food Pyramid. Recommended monthly consumption of gray matter is approximately 3 pounds, or half a brain per sitting. Note that the upper spine is also considered part of the Brain Group.

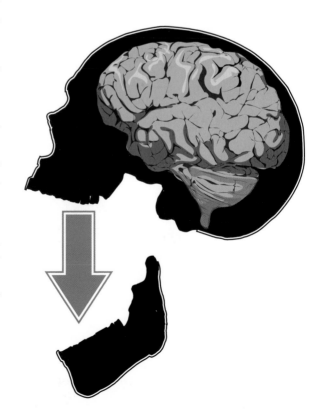

The brain of your victim will be protected by the skull. However, once you remove his or her lower jaw, it can easily be accessed. As stated earlier, eating a brain will give you a medulla rush, increasing your mobility with a burst of adrenaline. For up to 24 hours after consuming brain, zombies are capable of running and jumping, which will improve their hunting and attacking skills.

Internal Organ Group

The heart, lungs, liver, pancreas, intestines, and other organs in the chest and abdomen are all suitable for eating. However, unlike organs in the Brain Group, your monthly intake should be 8–10 pounds, or roughly 144 ounces. That's a couple lungs, a few hearts, and a liver or two. So depending on the number of zombies in your horde, you will need multiple bodies to fulfill your internal organ requirement. Alternatively, feedings from this group can be replaced with additional servings from the Brain or Blood Groups.

Most of the gooey goodies in the Internal Organ Group are protected by your victim's rib cage. Though it is not difficult to break the rib cage, you can just as easily reach under the ribs and extract the organs by hand.

Blood Group

It is essential to keep your body hydrated in order to absorb much-needed energy from uninfected flesh. Human blood is an excellent source of hydration.

Unlike vampires, who are obsessed with sucking, you can consume blood simply by eating flesh—the living human body uses blood to transport nutrients and oxygen to every cell in the body. Full-sized adults contain an average of 5.3 quarts of blood, making up roughly 7 percent of their body weight. This represents about two-thirds of your recommended monthly allowance. However, it's virtually impossible to extract that amount of blood from a single human in one sitting.

Don't be concerned about mixing blood types (A, B, AB, O). Consumption of incompatible blood types will not cause complications, though it has been observed that type O blood can give you the shakes.

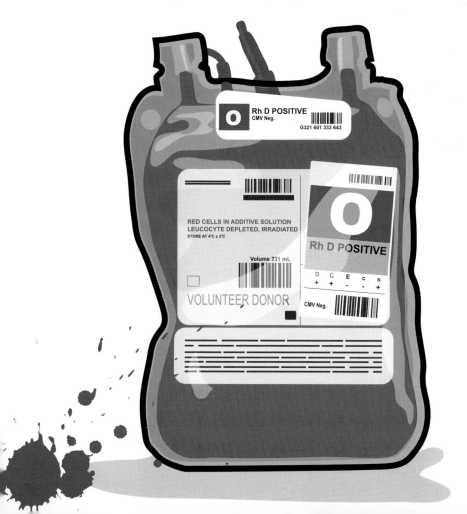

Bone Marrow Group

The Bone Marrow Group, also known as the Table Scrap Group, is typically what is left after a hungry horde fully consumes a body. The human body should have 206 bones, each one filled with red and yellow marrow. This marrow is made up of juicy blood cells. For minimal nutrition, we suggest 10–20 servings, though optimal nutrition is much higher—30–40 servings.

Servings from the Bone Marrow Group can be replaced by additional servings from the Brain or Blood Group, if available— that's what you really crave, after all. But leftover marrow will keep you on your feet until you have an opportunity to hunt down something more satisfying.

Bone marrow can be difficult to extract, but try to avoid stuffing full bones into your body. Bones such as the femur (the thigh bone) are large and can cause complications in your absorption tract. Finger and toes, on the other hand, can be consumed whole.

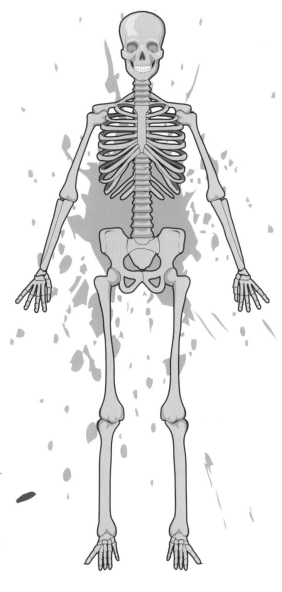

Feeding Etiquette

Proper zombie feeding etiquette can mean the difference between feasting on a fresh kill and foraging for rodents.

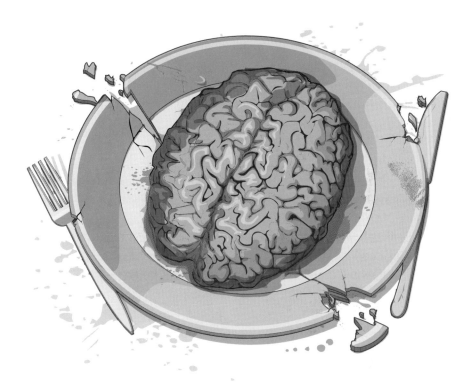

Don't Start Eating Until Your Victim Is Ready

Wounded humans will continually attempt to escape your clutches by fleeing or fighting. Even if they are experiencing early symptoms of z-virus infection, until paralysis sets in they are capable of inflicting damage.

So the first thing you must do before eating your victim is to continue inflicting trauma until your meal is unresponsive. The quickest method is blunt force to the head. Your victims' head. Not yours.

Never Play with Your Food

If your victim is unconscious, he or she may be experiencing the advanced stages of zombification. Procrastinating could result in your victim completing reanimation and shambling away. Once it becomes fast-on-its-feet food, you've forfeited your meal.

Even if reanimation is not forthcoming, an uneaten human can quickly attract other hungry zeds. As the Zombie Code states, everyone is entitled to a meal (see "The Zombie Code," page 143). The longer you wait, the less flesh for you. If the feeding frenzy becomes overwhelming, we suggest you remove one of the victim's limbs and creep away.

Rotten Is a No-No

In the panic of a zombie outbreak, humans often die from accidents, infighting, or other non-zombie-induced scenarios. As a result, you're likely to encounter unclaimed food in your wanderings. If you do stumble upon a meal just lying around, it may have passed its expiration date. Any lifeless carcass, simmering and swelling in the sun for longer than 12 to 16 hours, has sustained severe cellular damage and has no nutritional value. If the body is bloated, gray in color, stinky, or has a toe tag, it's a good indicator that it's been around a while.

During your rampaging haste, you may miss these warning signs. Fortunately, your body will automatically reject rotten meat. During zombification, the z-virus modified your tongue's taste receptors to detect and reject unproductive flesh. Try sinking your teeth into a bloated stomach—your body will instantly cease craving that particular torso.

If you ignore this warning and continue to chomp down on rotten flesh, you may suffer from absorption blockage. Symptoms may include upset stomach, abnormal vision, and increased projectile vomiting.

Use Your Mouth

Food should always enter your body through your mouth. This is the quickest path to your digestive tract. Some zeds may attempt to stuff human flesh directly into their open body cavities. This is not recommended. Although absorption is still possible, without a path out of the body this flesh becomes dead weight, decreasing your maneuverability.

Of course, even if you are missing a mouth or a stomach, you will still crave food. In this situation, first attempt to insert the flesh down your throat, but if this is impossible, go ahead and jam it into your body.

Absorption

While most species become sleepy while digestion takes place, the undead become more active during the absorption period, especially after they consume a human brain. This period of increased intensity can last up to 48 hours, while medulla rush capabilities (jumping and running) will last up to 24 hours. Both the surrounding temperature and tissue freshness can influence these times. The ideal temperature for absorption is around 78° F. If you are in a hot climate, we suggest that you wait for the temperature to drop at night before consuming anything.

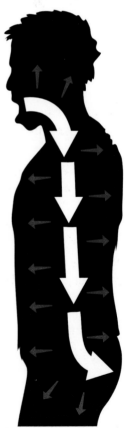

The z-virus will absorb everything except for hair, teeth, claws (finger- and toenails), and major bones. However, it will extract as much marrow as it can before excreting any waste. Depending on virus strain, complete absorption can take up to 48 hours.

After absorption is complete, your body will discard any waste within 24 hours, ideally through a relaxed sphincter. However, due to overeating or damage to your digestive tract, waste material can sometimes leave the body through gastric blowout. Abdominal ruptures eventually affect two out of three zombies, and 95 percent of boomer types (see "What's Your Body Type?" page 26). While embarrassing and disgusting, it really has no impact on your day-to-day functions. And yes, spilled waste is infectious for up to two days, depending on climate conditions.

Another complication to look out for is a body clog. When this happens, waste will continually build up in your body. Eventually, you'll be burdened with hundreds of pounds of unprocessed flesh, affecting your mobility and eventually ending your post-life.

Ordering Off the Menu

No question, human flesh is essential for a balanced diet, but what happens if the living aren't available? To avoid malnutrition during famine or post-apocalyptic conditions, turn to the hearty choices the animal kingdom has to offer. Many animals have internal organs similar to humans'. They are often slower and dumber than breathers but will yield more flesh and blood. Most of the multicellular species listed on the Hierarchy Hunting Chart below can provide basic sustenance, though rarely the complete nourishment human flesh provides. The farther up the chart you go, the better off you'll be.

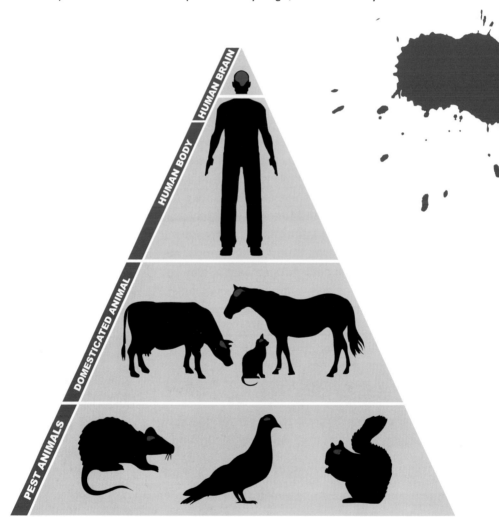

Larger animals such as livestock and house pets are fabulous human substitutes. Many of these creatures will be abandoned by their owners and weakened by starvation. Our experience shows that while canines can cause some bodily damage, their bites are rarely fatal (unlike ours).

Finally, there are rodents, birds, and small reptiles. These little critters make up a vast majority of animals found in most regions. High in numbers, they are still troublesome to catch, making them extremely annoying.

In certain areas, you may be tempted to hunt large primates like gorillas or chimpanzees. Yes, the DNA in these animals is almost 98 percent identical to a human's, and they could easily supplement your dietary needs. Yet despite their nutritional advantages, hunting great apes is not recommended. A gorilla can lift 10 times its own body weight, strength enough to rip a frail zed body to shreds. Plus, primates are capable of contracting the z-virus (see "Infecting Animals," page 132), and who wants the competition?

Other powerful animals such as bears, elephants, and large cats should also be avoided. Refer to the Animal Avoidance Chart below.

Oversized snakes have also been known to feed on zombies. If one swallows you whole, you will need to claw or bite your way out of its stomach. Even though the virus will kill the snake during the digestive process, you'll still be stuck inside a dead snake.

Other Foods to Avoid

With a hunger as unrelenting as yours, you may even feel the urge to snack on other substances beyond human and animal flesh. To be on the safe side, here are some you should steer clear of:

🕸 **Flammable Liquids.** Complex chemicals such as gasoline, acetone, and ethanol should never be consumed. These liquids have a high degree of flammability—they'll turn you into a quick-light zed! Other chemicals can also lead to increased decomposition. Items labeled with the following symbols are hazardous and should be avoided.

🕸 **Adhesives.** If someone has thrown a sticky compound on you, do not eat it! Although it may smell like horse or cow meat, it's not. More likely, it's designed to bond items together, things such as zombie jaws. If ingested, your body could eventually lock up. Handling an adhesive compound can also reduce your hands' dexterity.

🕸 **Polymers.** Plastic materials often have sharp edges that could damage your body during consumption. These and similar nonflesh materials— metal, glass, and wood—have no nutritional benefit. Humans sometimes use these materials as armor or jewelry; eat around them.

8

INFECTING

It's not just you—all zeds are infatuated with the living. After all, they are your only physical need. Obsessed as you are with feeding, it's not abnormal (relatively speaking) for you to turn a deaf ear to all other distractions. But while you're eating humans, you should also give some thought to recruiting them. After all, like most predators, zombies are stronger in numbers. The more zombies you walk with, the more humans you can kill and infect— which means still more zombies, and on and on!

Amazingly, as you hunt and battle humans, something magical happens: you will automatically transfer the z-virus to your opponents. Also known as the *zombie shot*, it's a simple fluid transfer that occurs during a bite or blood splatter. Once the virus is in a breather's bloodstream, the infection is irreversible.

Though you have completed your task, the newly infected human has just been introduced to a new world. The infected's first hours are the most critical. First, the zed-to-be must avoid being consumed. He or she will often flee from your attack, even as the early symptoms of the z-virus kick in. During the virus's incubation period, the victim's own bodily fluids become progressively more infectious; often an infected individual will seek shelter with other humans only to spread the virus to those in hiding. They will only welcome the stealth zed until obvious symptoms appear, at which point the infected human will be quarantined or destroyed. The good news is, the communicable seed has already been planted! Depending on the humans' health precautions and the virulence of the z-virus strain, this common scenario can lead to an impressive outbreak.

On the flip side, as mentioned in earlier chapters, it's very possible that a newly infected human will be so weakened by the virus that he or she is incapable of escaping your clutches. Good job—eat up! If your feeding frenzy does not damage your victim's cranial area, and the victim was still alive before the z-virus stopped his or her heart, reanimation as a zombie is still possible. Your new zed friend likely will be a bit dismantled, and not easy on the eyes, but who among the undead is?

In other words, if you continue to properly hunt and attack, your horde should grow without any extra effort on your part. What's better than getting something for nothing? However, if you have a rabid itch to maximize your infectious potential, this chapter is for you.

Administering an Infection

Most zombies are very reluctant to exert themselves by actively trying to infect a human. They really don't care! Behavior like this may seem lazy, but it's to be expected. Zombies may mob together, but they're mostly independent. We certainly wouldn't expect you to sacrifice a meal for the greater good of the apocalyptic pandemic! However, in every zed's post-life comes a time when it is overwhelmed with meal choices. At that moment, when the human supply seems like more than you can handle, why not use your built-in biological weapons to weaken the resistance?

The most common way to transmit the z-virus is to expose your victim to your infected bodily fluids. The human body is covered with entry points that are vulnerable to viral penetration. The eyes, mouth, nose, and ears are all potential gateways to the human circulatory system. So are uncovered wounds anywhere on the body. More exotic infection methods, such as injection via syringe, have also been reported.

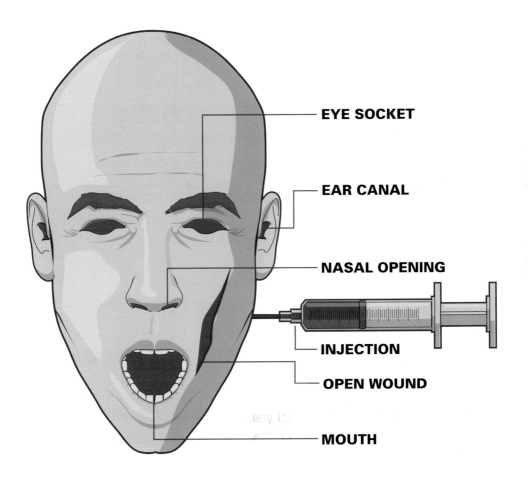

EYE SOCKET

EAR CANAL

NASAL OPENING

INJECTION

OPEN WOUND

MOUTH

To increase your chances of infection, use one of the popular transfer methods outlined below.

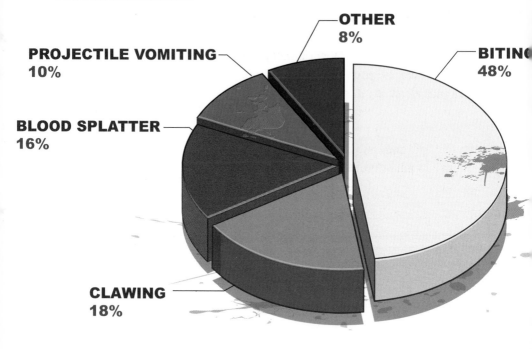

OTHER
8%

PROJECTILE VOMITING
10%

BLOOD SPLATTER
16%

BITING
48%

CLAWING
18%

Bite It!

What did you say? "Bite me"? No problem! Forty-eight percent of all zombies were infected through a bite. As you already know, your mouth is like a versatile Swiss army knife. You can use it for attacking, holding, feeding, moaning—and infecting, too. Once your rotten grill breaks the skin of a living human, they're contaminated. No wonder the zombie jaw is so feared by humans.

Cranial bites are the most effective, though humans will often block your attempts with their hands. A few fingers in your mouth shouldn't stop you—think of them as appetizers. Unfortunately, if your fingerless target does make it to reanimation, the new recruit may be of little use in a fight. Without opposable thumbs, how will it ever use a melee weapon?

Clawing

A less serious but still very effective means
of transference is administered through
your knifelike fingernails. Any lacerations
on a living body caused by scratching will
be vulnerable to your infectious blood.
Once your victim is infected, z-virus symptoms will increase his or her vulnerability,
including numbness around the infected
scratch. Of course, too much clawing
can lead to potentially fatal blood loss . . .
which is fine if you are hungry.

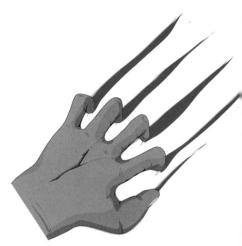

Blood Splatter

The third most common means of transference is the
infamous psycho blood splatter. This method is less
controllable than biting or scratching, but it frequently
occurs during altercations with the living. If one of your
body parts is crushed or cut by a breather's attack,
infected blood may fly from your body or the attacker's
weapon and land on a human's skin.

However, because you do not have a functioning
circulatory system like a human, your blood will not
spray when an artery is cut. It needs to enter an open
wound or facial opening through its own momentum.

Projectile Vomiting

Records show that exposure to infected vomit
is the forth leading cause of infection. As with
blood splatter, the vomit will need to penetrate
a wound or facial opening if it is to infect your
victim. Depending on what is churning in that
stomach of yours, it's easily possible to produce a half-gallon of heave. With that much
spew, you can quickly infect an entire group
of last-ditch defenders. Hopefully they are
shocked, standing with their mouths open.

Other Methods

It's amazing how many atypical sources of infections we have observed. They're rarely the result of zed action, but it's still good to be aware of the possibilities. Breathers can contract the z-virus by consuming infected food or being bitten by a mosquito that has recently fed on infected blood. Human scientists may inject test subjects with the virus for research purposes. We have even witnessed a newly infected human purposely infecting friends and family for undead companionship.

Of all the bizarre viral vectors, sexual contact is most common. After close encounters with our forces, human survivors tend to feel a heightened need for physical and emotional intimacy. It isn't uncommon for the opposition to lay down their arms for a bit, and lie down with each other. As mentioned before, early symptoms of the virus are not always visible, with or without clothing.

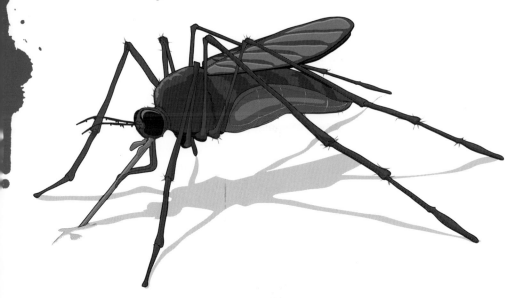

DID YOU KNOW?

The z-virus is capable of surviving during an organ transplant. Once the organ is introduced into a new body, the patient can quickly become infected.

Stages of Zombification

The act of transference was child's play compared to the process of zombification. Every zombie goes through a series of uncomfortable transformations that lead to reanimation. Incubation times vary, but with the most common strain of the z-virus, the process takes about 24 hours. If you are curious about what actually happens during transformation and reanimation, review the seven stages of zombification below.

Stage 1: Infection

Isn't it amazing that this microscopic devil is the foundation of the undead kingdom? With millions of viruses, why is the z-virus the most feared by man? First off, it's resilient. The armored capsid is capable of fending off 100 percent of antiviral drugs developed by human science. In addition, the z-virus is fast! It does not discriminate based on age, size, race, or method of transference, and will take only seconds to bypass the immune system and begin zed restoration. Once introduced into the bloodstream, the virus dedicates itself to reproduction (yeah, baby!) and quickly begins to self-assemble within host cells.

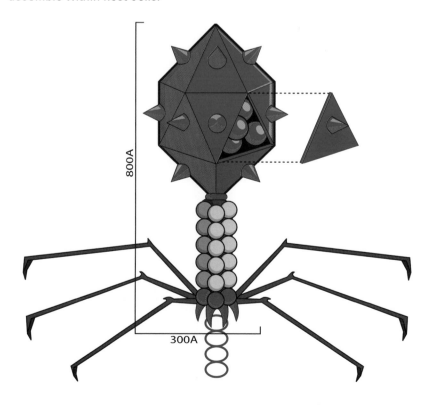

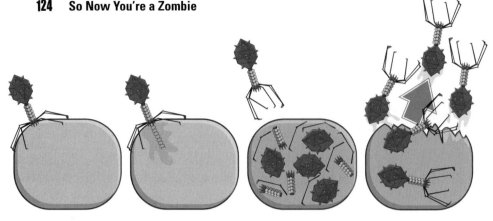

Within 20 seconds, all of the body's thousands of miles of veins will flow with infected blood. At this point, the circulatory system is only helping the virus. Unaware of the invasion, it will continue to cycle blood throughout the entire body, roughly three times every minute. This makes amputation of an infected limb almost impossible; a victim would have only seconds to remove the appendage, and that's a procedure the living prefer not to rush.

As the virus attacks and breaks down healthy blood plasma, the human's blood begins to coagulate. Eventually the heart will experience complications from the coagulating blood, prompting it to increase the number of beats per minute. This produces the z-virus's first symptom: high blood pressure. Amazingly, the resulting pressure is forceful enough to squirt blood up to 30 feet, assuming the still-functioning heart is lacerated correctly.

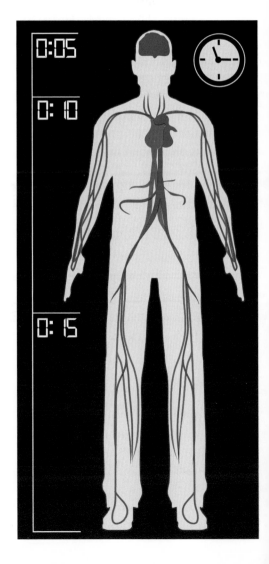

The coagulating blood also causes signs of rigor mortis in the victim's muscles. Other early signs of infection include skin discoloration, pain, and numbness. The skin will attempt to combat the infection, and will turn a purplish-brown color. The nervous system reacts to the unpleasant sensory overload; twitching and cursing are common.

Stage 2: Fever

With the human immune system incapable of stopping the infection, more visible symptoms begin to appear. Although the victim experiences chills, his or her internal body temperature actually elevates, showing signs of a high-grade fever of around 100 to 106° F. The fever will continue to worsen until the paralysis of stage 4 sets in. The chart below should give you an idea of the progression.

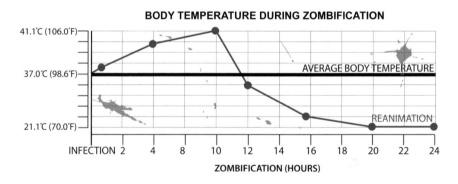

BODY TEMPERATURE DURING ZOMBIFICATION

Increased heart rate will lead to acute joint pain, and the victim's body will try to counteract the attack by vomiting. Stomach fluids and undigested food have a high probability of being infectious at this stage, making the victim's vomit lethal.

Stage 3: Early Brain Mutation

The host's cognitive functions are severely damaged as the virus begins to infest the billions of neurons in the brain. Severe encephalitis (inflammation of the brain) causes confusion and abnormal behavior. Cells that are not mutated are often killed in the process.

Hallucinations and mild dementia are followed by the inability to speak or swallow. The operation of individual neurons is disrupted, impairing mus-cle coordination and ultimately leading to partial paralysis. The virus also

alters the brain's thalamus, shutting down all pain receptors, and damages the temporal lobe. Once these renovations are complete, the victim will be capable only of basic motor functions and primitive instinctual responses.

Stage 4: Paralysis

Full-body paralysis is necessary in order to restrain the body during the final stages of transformation. A body that does not lose complete mobility could overexert itself, possibly causing permanent death (i.e., no post-life).

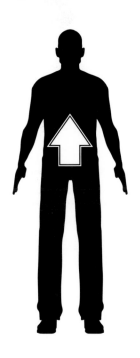

In the paralysis stage, the victim first experiences overall numbness as the virus lowers his or her heart rate. Then lower-body paralysis sets in, followed by upper-body paralysis. The victim's flesh is now 50 percent infectious, and it generates reduced levels of the once-irresistible fresh-flesh pheromone (see "Nose," page 24). So not only is the host's flesh becoming useless to you and your fellow hungry zombies, but it will also repel you from attacking. This is a helpful feature, because if the victim is attacked and killed before reaching the final stages of zombification, he or she will never make it to reanimation.

Stage 5: Coma

While it appears that the body has shut down, the virus is actually modifying the nanotubes in the host's cellular walls. Once these structures are completely infected and transformed, they transport endogenous chemicals from cell to cell, allowing low-level intercellular communication that bypasses the complex systems of the human body. While this cellular communication is slower, it is necessary once the victim's nervous system shuts down.

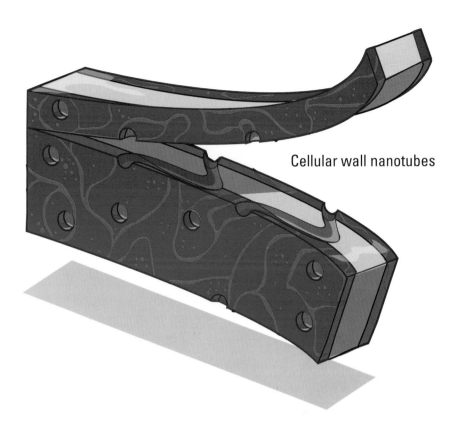

Cellular wall nanotubes

More zed puberty is also taking place. Skeletal muscles are slightly modified to serve basic locomotion. These muscles no longer need oxygen-rich blood; instead, they function with the blood already circulating in the muscles at the time of infection. This infected blood eventually will need to be replenished by uninfected flesh.

Stage 6: Heart Stoppage

A necessary step of zombification is to disconnect all energy-draining body functions. Once cell mutation is complete, the virus pulls the plug—like you, the victim is now a flatliner! Once the heart stops, brain activity also comes to a screeching halt, erasing his or her memory.

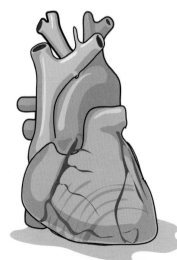

Stage 7: Reanimation

What's up, zombification survivor? The host's anatomy now experiences reverse rigor mortis, unclamping the body following its final transformation. This reanimation can take anywhere from a few minutes to several hours, depending on virus strain. Body temperature levels off at approximately 70° F, and low-level viral brain activity can also be detected.

The new zombie will start to experience faint body movements that are stimulated by reflexes. It will eventually arise to discover a combination of physical and psychological changes, along with new abilities with which it is not yet familiar. Subconsciously, it feels hungry, not in the stomach but in the brain. This is the virus communicating that it needs human flesh . . . *now*! The victim is now 100 percent infected, and one bad-ass zed!

Worldwide Infection

Any brain-eating zed currently roaming the earth has the potential to fully contaminate the world of the living. No matter how an outbreak spreads, its all starts with one zombie—maybe even you! If you have the ambition to be Patient Zero, you must first squeeze out a teaspoon of infected blood and get yourself to a highly popu-

lated area for about 30 days. Your main goal should be to quickly decrease the number of the breathers while increasing the infected horde.

For a better understanding of what a worldwide outbreak would look like, we've created a best-case model covering 160 days. It clearly demonstrates your infectious potential. However, many factors, such as population density, geography, and the effectiveness of the human resistance could alter the real-world results. Remember, zed plans never go according to plan, so be prepared for the unexpected.

8 Days

Someone's been infected! Perhaps thanks to you, the first humans have suc-cumbed to the z-virus and withstood zombification. Initial success isn't just dumb luck; as mentioned before, we rely on the fact that the newly infected are often misdiagnosed and not properly treated with preventative termina-tion. For this reason, three out of five new zombies survive the first 48 hours, and 56 percent of all outbreaks last at least 8 days.

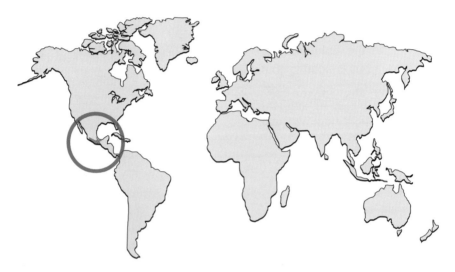

Once reanimated and unrestrained, the new recruits are free to quickly disrupt the human status quo. Remember, without aggressive networking, the horde's effort will simply fizzle out. If you want to maintain a terrifying crisis level, we suggest you infect 75 humans during the outbreak's incuba-tion period. Yes, this sounds daunting, but with a 24-hour reanimation cycle, you won't be working alone for long.

30 Days

If the outbreak has survived the first 30 days, it has a real chance. At this point, zombie numbers should have escalated into the thousands. A horde this size is very capable of generating widespread panic. The living resis-tance will scramble to quarantine large metropolitan areas within military perimeters. With high-density populations trapped, the infection will spread rapidly.

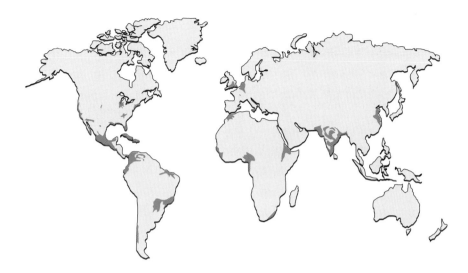

Cities and small countries have the potential to collapse altogether, sometimes in as short as 28 days. To further spread the outbreak, you'll need to penetrate containment perimeters. Review previous chapters for information on how to navigate obstacles and barricades.

160 Days

If the outbreak is still raging after 160 days, containment perimeters have clearly been compromised. A global pandemic is now within reach. With multiple fronts battling a worldwide outbreak, humans will show signs of

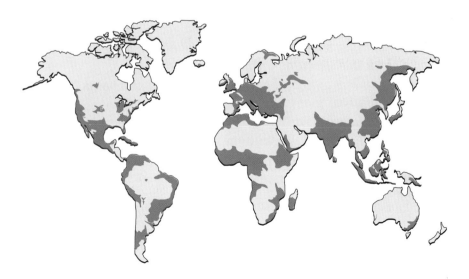

exhaustion, their supplies diminished. Soon even larger countries may be overrun by hundreds of thousands of hungry brain-eaters.

The infected horde will continue to multiply unless new, unconventional weaponry is successfully deployed against the horde. To prevent such a setback, targeting the humans' high-tech installations becomes increasingly important (see "Other Human Infrastructures," page 58). Toward the tail-end of the first year of infection, the total collapse of human civilization will be near. With any luck, you could soon be walking through the valley of the shadow of death, fearing no evil!

Reset your calendars to 1 A.Z.—After Zombie!

Infecting Animals [NOT RECOMMENDED]

Depending on z-virus strain and their own biological makeup, some animals can experience zombification. The following creatures are the most susceptible to infection: apes, bears, bulls, cats, chimps, crocodiles, crows, dogs, elephants, gorillas, hippopotamuses, horses, komodo dragons, monkeys, pigs, rhinos, sharks, and wolves. A pretty impressive lineup—so would it be a good idea to invite infected critters into the horde?

The real question is, why risk it? Animals that resemble something out of a Pet Sematary are never a good idea to have around, not even for zombies. Think about it: if infected, an animal with far superior speed and strength would be competing with zeds to consume human flesh, and would likely succeed! In addition, attempting to purposely infect an animal can end in your own disfigurement. Almost all zombified animals are uncontrollable. And some animals, because of their size and power, should be avoided, infected or not (see "Ordering Off the Menu," page 114).

Only a few undead animal could realistically assist a horde. The most notable is zed's best friend, the domesticated zombie canine. (Not to be confused with werezombies.) But infected dogs are susceptible to many of the same problems zeds face; they need uninfected flesh to hold back the ravages of decomposition. They also have a shorter life cycle than human brain-eaters, due to the increased physical strain their undead bodies are subjected to.

It's also surprisingly difficult to deliberately infect even a domesticated animal. If captured, most animals will reject your toxic flesh as food. The zed body certainly doesn't smell appetizing, and it lacks carbohydrates, fats, and proteins. Starving animals that foolishly consume infectious flesh often die and do not reanimate.

But as with humans, animal are sometimes infected unintentionally. A curious critter that sniffs infected poo-poo or a terminated zed corpse could pick up the strain. (By the same token, if an uninfected human sniffs around an infected animal corpse, he or she could be infected.) Animals can also contract the virus by attacking a zombie—but that doesn't mean it's a good idea to deliberately provoke an animal in order to infect it!

9

IN THE END

Change is in the stale air—or is it the absence of that sweet fragrance of flesh? Sprawling streets, once filled with ear-piercing screams and sirens, are now mute, save only for the howl of the wind. Juicy bodies have been replaced with useless rotten carcasses. Ruination is everywhere, with barricades unbreached, a sure sign of death. Either by depletion or evacuation, once-plentiful brainy resources have all but disappeared, and your monthly supply of grub has become murderous to round up.

What's worse, the once relentless horde is beginning to show signs of fragility. Starving zeds go stiff from extreme decomposition. The z-virus may have mutated, removing the very safeguards that once kept one zombie from attacking another. As the violence grows, snapping and clawing gives way to zed-on-zed murder.

Is this it? Is this the zombie plague we so desperately pursued? Are you feeling like the unwitting pawn in an undead apocalypse?

Well, if you think the end is near, read on.

Never Give Up!

Yes, you heard us right: never give up! Intoxicating gray matter may be hard to scare up, but it's out there, waiting to be slurped down. While the human race may seem fragile, history has proven that they show amazing perseverance. No matter how overwhelming the zed siege was, pockets of mortals may survive in hiding, camouflaged, conspiring toward yet another undead onslaught.

To find these hidden breathers, may we suggest a change of scenery? Shamble your horde to new, unfamiliar hunting grounds. Do whatever is necessary to prolong your post-life along the way, including taste-testing nonhuman sources of food (see "Ordering Off the Menu," page 114). Experiment with all types of creepy-crawly foods, including worms and bugs.

No matter how desperate you are, though, do not resort to zombie cannibalism! Unless you're doing it for some twisted personal revenge, eating a fellow zed serves absolutely no purpose, and is actually counterproductive. Infected flesh does not nourish the z-virus; it will only weigh down your frame, reducing your mobility. In addition, if you introduce an incompatible virus strain into your body, there could be all types of unpleasant side effects, including virus blisters. These pockets of toxic fluids can reduce your zombie abilities—eyes, ears, nose, and mouth can become clogged with skin boils. So before sampling another zed, search under every rock, leaf, and twig for an edible alternative. And rest assured that your tasty human opposition is out there somewhere, ready to be put back on the menu.

"Well-done apocalyptic is better than well-said apocalyptic."
—ZEDJAMIN FRANKLIN

Escaping Captivity

As a zombie outbreak winds down, you may find yourself captured by the elusive human resistance. While you probably won't be happy to find yourself quarantined, it's better than decapitation any day.

Keep in mind, however, that the breathers didn't spare your life out of the goodness of their still-beating hearts. They generally capture zombies to engage in experimentation and tingling torture, neither of which should faze you. But another possibility is that they are processing you for disposal, which *will* faze you—out!

Humans are fully aware that you pose a serious hazard to them. To keep you safely contained, they'll often resort to shackles and solitary confinement. Imprisoned, away from the horde, what's a zed to do?

Step 1: Gnaw on Your Restraints

Your first move should be to free yourself from bondage. Use your teeth. Leather, plastic, and rope can all be gnawed through. But if the restraints are made out of a metal alloy, you may need to chew or twist off your appendages. Don't get carried away—just gnaw the appendages that are restrained. Yes, dismemberment sucks, but at least you'll be one step (or crawl) closer to freedom.

Step 2: Attack the Guards

Use one of your body weapons (see "Use Your Body as a Weapon," page 81) to overcome your captors. Projectile vomiting is the most effective weapon when confined, but it's not always possible for all zeds. Continue kicking and screaming until you've released your deadly contagion onto one or all of your captors.

Step 3: Exit

If the previous step succeeds, your living guards soon should be feeling the symptoms of the virus. This gives you a few exit options:

🕱 You can try to bolt while they are weakened and delusional—however, you may run into obstacles (see "Obstacles You Will Face," page 59).

☣ You can wait until the virus paralyzes them, feed on them for strength, and then attempt to depart.

☣ Perhaps the best option is to wait for your captors to be reanimated. If they survive zombification, they may be a big help. Research from field observation has shown that some newly reanimated zeds repeat past learned behaviors, such as unlocking cell doors. Your new zedmate could very well set you free!

Zombicide

Zombicide (*ZOM-bee-side*): The act of voluntarily terminating oneself, if one is a zombie, during an activity that does not involve pursuing human flesh.

Desperate times call for desperate measures. When all else fails, some zeds may want to avoid a slow, decomposing death. While we do not advocate zombicide, we can't stop you from trying it. You may have encountered too many hazards in the human world, any of which could have terminated you. But what if no mortal is present to do the deed? Two self-inflicted options stand out from all the others. Review these options, but please reconsider—you have your whole undead life ahead of you!

Fire

After any widespread zombie uprising, you're likely to find a number of fires burning out of control. If you are a truly lazy zed, and are suffering the drying effects of decomposition, creep into the burning embers to end it all. The next few minutes will be your last, as flames swallow up your devilish bag of bones.

Fall

Height can kill! If you're looking for a quick way to destroy your brain, take a tumble off a bridge, parking structure, or high-rise. But before you do, make sure you'll be falling three stories or more. Anything less will just cause deformities.

Be warned, other zeds may follow you. Zombies have been known to exhibit lemming-like behavior, which could turn your zombicide into a deadly game of follow the leader. To reduce horde fatalities, wait until your fellow zombies are safely out of sight.

APPENDIX

THE ZOMBIE CODE

In the early part of the first century A.D., the zombie movement was plagued with setbacks. Operating without guidelines or responsibilities, our predecessors' mismanaged terror campaign only led to the demise of a number of zombie hordes. Eventually, they decided to draw up a simple Undead Agreement, known today as the Zombie Code. This code outlines general rules of behavior for the undead.

Unfortunately, many new recruits are unaware of this document. We provide it here as a public service.

I. A zombie shall hunt, fight, and feed on the living.

II. All zombies shall have equal title to fresh provisions, even if they do not take part in the capture or kill.

III. A zombie shall engage in battle with any humans it encounters, whatever the odds. Those who do not are guilty of cowardice, which is punishable by decapitation.

IV. A zombie on fire shall always run directly toward humans, avoiding all other undead.

V. No zombie shall intentionally take a blow to protect another zombie; this show of emotion will lead to decapitation.

VI. A zombie shall not sleep or rest under any circumstances.

VII. A zombie that loses a limb during an engagement shall be given half a brain in compensation.

VIII. No zombie shall speak or attempt to speak any coherent words. If a zombie does, its blue tongue will be removed.

IX. All zombies shall have the right to engage in zed-on-zed violence.

X. A zombie shall work toward the complete destruction of the living, helping to transform the living landscape into the kingdom of the undead.

XI. A zombie shall never follow the laws of man, punishable by decapitation.

After reviewing these articles, you must now swear to them by moaning a garbled affirmation to the following oath:

I solemnly swear that I will uphold and defend the Zombie Code against all enemies, living and robotic; that I will bear true faith and allegiance to the zombie apocalypse; that I will perform all duties cursed upon me as a warrior of the undead. I take this obligation against my free will.

Only after you have incoherently sworn to uphold your duties will the undead horde accept you. Your body is now the property of the zombie movement. As a member, your responsibilities will be modest but important. Should you want to be released from this obligation, you may do so through decapitation.

FINAL WORD

A MESSAGE FOR THE LIVING

So, you living bastard, this zombie handbook has found its way into your juicy hands? Think you've uncovered the secrets of the walking undead? Think again! The pages of this book have been laced with the z-virus. You're now enrolled, either through finger-to-nose or finger-to-mouth transference. At this very moment, the virus is incubating in your body. Symptoms will soon begin to show.

There is no known cure. Welcome to the army of the undead. By reading and possessing this book, you have now received the information necessary to wipe out the rest of the human race. Thank you for joining us in one of the greatest conflicts in zed history!

Also from Chicago Review Press

MiniWeapons of Mass Destruction

Build Implements of Spitball Warfare

John Austin

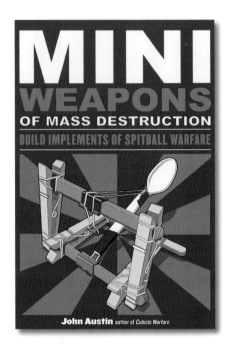

We've come a long way from the Peashooter Era! Using items that can be found in the modern junk drawer, troublemakers of all stripes have the components they need to assemble an impressive arsenal of miniaturized weaponry.

MiniWeapons of Mass Destruction provides fully illustrated step-by-step instructions for building 35 projects, including:

- Clothespin Catapult
- Clip Crossbow
- Matchbox Bomb
- Coin Shooter
- Shoelace Darts

- Hanger Slingshot
- Paper-Clip Trebuchet
- Ping-Pong Zooka
- Tube Launcher
- And more!

And for those who are more MacGyver than marksman, *MiniWeapons* also includes target designs, from aliens to zombies, for practice in defending their personal space.

256 pages • 6 x 9 • paper • $16.95 (CAN $18.95) • 978-1-55652-953-5

Distributed by IPG
www.ipgbook.com

www.chicagoreviewpress.com

Available at your favorite bookstore,
(800) 888-4741, or www.chicagoreviewpress.com